Brain
Training
for Dogs

Brain Training for Dogs

Cognitive Games and **Activities** to **Unlock Your Pet's Full Potential**

CLAIRE ARROWSMITH

Michael O'Mara Books Limited

First published in Great Britain in 2024 by
Michael O'Mara Books Limited
9 Lion Yard
Tremadoc Road
London SW4 7NQ

A CIP catalogue record for this book is available from the British
Library.

Papers used by Michael O'Mara Books Limited are natural, recyclable
products made from wood grown in sustainable forests. The
manufacturing processes conform to the environmental regulations of
the country of origin.

ISBN: 978-1-78929-604-4 in paperback print format
ISBN: 978-1-78929-605-1 in ebook format

1 2 3 4 5 6 7 8 9 10

Designed and typeset by Design 23
Illustrations by Peter Liddiard
Cover design by Natasha Le Coultre
Cover photos from shutterstock.com

Printed and bound by CPI Group (UK) Ltd, Croydon, CR0 4YY

www.mombooks.com

MIX
Paper | Supporting
responsible forestry
FSC® C171272

CONTENTS

INTRODUCTION

Dogs have been our companions through some of the most exciting stages of our evolutionary existence. As a result, they have a unique place in the lives of many of us, and as species we are inexplicably connected. Having said this, we are still learning about what makes our four-legged friends tick. As our knowledge about learning, welfare, ethics and cognition grows, dogs continue to be of constant focus and fascination to us. Attitudes to dog ownership are constantly shifting and the motivation to ensure our dogs have the very best of existences has never been stronger.

Part of this effort to forge deeper bonds and to fulfil the needs of our dogs involves the importance of utilizing and satisfying the mental requirements of our pets that we are becoming increasingly aware of. The aim of this book is to help further our awareness of a dog's cognitive abilities and to provide ideas about how we can maximize our enjoyment from time spent with our dogs. Gone are the days where repeatedly tossing a ball is considered sufficiently entertaining; in fact, increasing evidence has shown us that this game, which is embedded in the mind of everyone who has ever encountered a dog, can be surprisingly problematic. However, considering so many of us remember apparently happy dogs who experienced exactly that kind of life, is it really necessary to do more?

Most of us want to live alongside our dogs enjoying the pleasure of having their company. There is little time to become canine scientists, and perhaps limited time to find the motivation when our modern lives are so busy. I hope with this book to help you discover just how amazing that dog sitting beside you really is, providing inspiration for activities that aim to benefit both you and your pet in several different ways.

The number of dogs living as companions in our homes has grown. While we are becoming less reliant on dogs as working tools, we need them in our lives as friends, a means to a healthier routine and for a level of emotional support that can be invaluable. Given this importance, it makes sense that we increasingly want to do right by them, to show our appreciation and recognition, and help them lead long and fulfilling lives.

WHAT MAKES A SUCCESSFUL CANINE COMPANION?

Dogs are a very special part of so many human lives and when we bring a dog into our home we are enthusiastic and optimistic about the role they will play. However, the rise of companion dog ownership has been accompanied by a rise in the demand for rescue shelter places, and both behavioural and training support, since things often don't quite go to plan. So it's important to focus on nurturing a positive and fulfilling experience for both your pet and you to ensure the experience is a good one for each of you. Let's take a look at what's really important when it comes to your relationship with your dog.

Successful communication

Understanding what our dogs are communicating is critical. They are highly perceptive to our cues and body language, but we need to make an effort to learn the meaning behind their signalling. By doing so, and understanding their emotional states, you can avoid potential mistakes and make decisions that benefit your dog most. This includes being able to understand how they are responding to your game training.

Essential socialization

While dogs have evolved to have an affinity towards humans, in order for them to live in our busy and chaotic world, they need to have sufficient early exposure to a range of environments, social encounters, animals, sounds and so on; the earlier the brain experiences these things the more likely the dog is to grow up feeling confident and resilient. If you have an adult dog that missed out on early socialization, then keep this in mind when you present them with new situations and tasks. Work within their capabilities and grow their confidence from there.

Creating consistency

Dogs thrive on having a routine that they understand. Every day does not need to be a carbon copy of the previous one, but having predictability in the provision of exercise, stimulation, sleep, meals and care helps. If you want to have house rules for your dog, such as not being permitted on furniture, or permitted to jump up when greeting, then stick by them; changing from one day to the next is confusing and can create anxiety. Knowing that games and training with you are always fun and never scary or stressful is also essential.

Positive interactions

This includes the positive reinforcement training methods recommended in this book. It has been shown that this approach fosters stronger and more trusting relationships between people and their dogs. Play and praise, both integral components of all the activities within these pages, promote lasting trust and cooperation.

Physical and mental stimulation

Appropriate access to exercise, mental activity and social interaction all contribute to a fulfilled lifestyle that will benefit your dog and help them to behave in desirable ways. Hopefully the games in this book will contribute to each of these areas.

Strong bonds

People who spend more time with their dog and engage in training report having stronger bonds. Having shared positive experiences and successes during activities means you get to know one another and develop trust.

WHAT IS CANINE COGNITION?

Since the 1960s, interest in animal cognition, neuro-science and learning theory has been growing and our skill in asking the right research questions has improved. We now have whole departments focused on canine cognition, and trainers no longer focus on just what our dogs can physically do, but also on how they are taught and the underlying emotions involved.

Canine cognition is a term that refers to the complete mental-processing capabilities exhibited by dogs. Dogs are unique due to the influence of their distinctive domestication process and therefore possess instincts and interactions that distinguish them from other animals, even other canid species. We continue to learn about the abilities of our closest companions, including their sensory perception, learning, memory, problem-solving and social behaviour skills.

Research is exposing our dog's ability to problem-solve to obtain rewards via solving mazes and puzzles, and by manipulating objects. We are increasingly aware of the complexity of the canine social experience and that our dogs are particularly capable of communicating not just with each other but with humans in ways that many other species cannot; they understand our gestures, body language and even facial expressions. There is evidence of observational learning where the dog imitates other dogs and humans in order to solve a problem, and some believe that dogs possess a form of 'theory of mind', which refers to the ability to attribute mental states and recognize oneself. All pretty complex and fascinating insights into the way our best friends think.

SHOULD I TRAIN MY DOG?

Research has shown that being *trainable* has a positive connection with longevity in your dog. Dogs that have regular attention and interaction with their people tend to receive medical attention earlier; it's much easier to detect early stages of problems when you are in close proximity and know your dog's responses keenly. Likewise, those dogs tend to have routines involving more exercise and more social contact, which result in improved communication and bonding with their families. Brains benefit significantly from being kept engaged; mental activity uses a wide range of areas and active neurons are more resilient to the impact of ageing (the old 'use it or lose it' adage). As with humans, there is strong evidence that participating in enjoyable activities provides protection against negative emotional difficulties too.

On a day-to-day basis, activities and mental stimulation can help to create a more balanced routine for your dog so that they don't experience boredom and frustration or have too much energy to burn at the wrong time. This helps to avoid many annoying behavioural habits from developing and can help in the management of already present problems. Having said this, it is important to recognize that being kept super-busy all the time is not ideal either. Each dog has their ideal balance of rest and activity and it is by getting to know them that we can understand the perfect routine.

CAN MY DOG DO THIS?

You might be starting this book while looking dubiously at your furry companion. Are they really that smart? While you know of super-smart dogs, is *this one* really that able? Of course! All dogs have potential and all dogs can adapt to, and engage with, their environment. We sometimes feel frustrated when our dogs don't appear to recall the training lesson we were working on yesterday, but this is usually because we have somehow confused the lesson, not practised it enough with different distractions or simply haven't thought through what is possible for our dog in this particular situation. All dogs are remarkable and the challenge set for you in this book is to explore as much of your dog's abilities as possible while building the strongest relationship you can.

Of course, not all dog–human relationships work out. Resolving some of the challenges that arise in dogs living alongside us requires more than just playing games. If your dog is displaying behaviour that is of concern to you, it is always advisable to discuss this with your veterinarian, who can refer you to a qualified practitioner. They can help you to understand your dog and to choose the activities that are most appropriate for your situation.

Perhaps you have recently acquired a dog from a rescue shelter and might wonder if games are appropriate for them. Many researchers have looked into why dogs end up being relinquished to shelters and a common conclusion is that behaviour and training difficulties are often top factors. Now that your new dog is home, they need time to learn about their new environment and to bond with their new family. Games and training are great ways to build those relationships, but do take things slowly so that your dog is never overwhelmed or confused; they may not be used to brain challenges or might have experienced some aversive training methods in the past, leaving them wary about what the new rules might be. Build the trust, get to know what they love, and the games can naturally develop afterwards.

HOW YOUR DOG EXPERIENCES THE WORLD

Remember that the world your dog perceives is rather different from ours. Their sensory system and processing is keenly developed to maximize their success as dogs, and at times we might have to remind ourselves that they are experiencing things we may not fully understand. These sensory abilities have been shaped by both their evolutionary history and, more recently, by the jobs we have selected them to perform.

Hearing

Have you noticed how mobile your dog's ears are? This makes them perfectly designed to accurately locate the sources of sound within a much broader range than humans, specifically in the higher-frequency region: 65 Hz to over 45,000 Hz (compared to our 20 Hz to 20,000 Hz). The lower range includes those we can detect as more like a slow vibration sensation than noise. The upper range is outside our capability to detect but creates an awareness of small prey animals, who use this range to communicate. Dogs can also detect sounds from some of our electronic devices that are inaudible to us. The auditory cortex in the canine brain is well developed to discriminate between different sound frequencies and to respond to the most subtle of noises.

Feeling dubious because your dog ignores your calls or is highly selective? Variations in ability do exist, with increased incidence of deafness occurring in some breeds (Dalmatians and Australian Cattle Dogs, for example) or decline in hearing due to illness or ageing.

Most of our dogs, however, hear well but choose what sounds are important to respond to based on past experience; so it might be time to change your cues if your dog is persistently ignoring you!

Olfaction

Your dog has an incredible capacity for detecting odour. Dogs live in a world of scent far outside our human range of perception, driven by their extensive number of olfactory receptors, which are estimated to be in the region of 225 million compared to our 6 million. They are specialists in scent discrimination and estimations state that they can detect odours at concentrations as low as parts per trillion (the best human noses tend to need parts per million).

All dogs have an advanced olfactory cortex in their brain to process the information gathered by their nose, and scent hounds have been shown to have an even greater brain area dedicated to this task. The dogs that we have bred for tracking and detection work have a remarkable ability to track missing persons, detect illegal substances, find explosives, identify diseases, locate buried objects, and perform search and rescue operations.

Not convinced because your dog seems to sometimes struggle to find things that are right in front of them? Sick of having to go and retrieve that ball yourself? Active searching is a focused, deliberate activity and an inexperienced or distracted dog might lack the concentration and approach to seek properly. Sometimes the dog is just not that motivated to find the item and will need some training to learn that search and find is highly rewarding. There are games in this book that will help you to develop those skills with your pet, so have a go.

Processing odours looks visibly different to normal relaxed breathing. Your dog will appear more focused on the area, may direct their head towards a specific area, drawing air into their nasal passages more quickly than before, sometimes appearing to taste the air. The three formal responses are tracking, trailing and air-scenting, each with their own strategy and ideal situation and therefore each used for the different jobs we employ dogs to do.

You might notice your dog rapidly pressing their tongue to the roof of their mouth, or chattering their teeth while salivating and raising their head. This unusual response is due to your dog pressing the odour molecules up to a specialized area situated in their palate behind the incisors. This is called the Jacobsen's or vomeronasal organ, which is designed to process special chemical messages called pheromones passed between dogs in urine and bodily secretions.

Vision

Dogs do not rely upon keen visual perception in the way that humans do as they don't need to see fine detail or read the small print on labels. They do not, as is sometimes thought, see in black and white, but instead have dichromatic colour vision (meaning that they see the world primarily in blue and yellow tones), as they have far fewer colour receptors than we do. Your dog's eyes are highly sensitive to detecting movement and they have a wider field of view than us; both designs make them a successful predator species.

Your dog's head shape will influence their range of vision: flat-faced breeds, with eyes positioned towards the front, have a more similar range to humans and those with longer noses and eyes set further around the side of the head experience a greater peripheral view.

Do your snapshots of your gorgeous, happy dog turn out with demonic, glowing eyes? There is a reflective layer behind their retina that enhances their ability to see in low-light conditions; very useful for them, but it can be a little frustrating when it reflects our camera flash right back at us.

Taste

Your dog's sense of taste is very functional and not particularly refined for a wide range of flavours. They rely on their sense of smell primarily but have evolved to avoid any potentially harmful substances by detecting bitterness. Having said that, dogs will taste or consume things that appear absolutely abhorrent to us, such as old carcasses, animal faeces and of course those treats they buried in the garden last year and have just recovered to gnaw on.

Taste receptors exist in and around your dog's mouth area, with numbers varying between breeds and individuals. They can detect the basic range of tastes: sweet, sour, salty, bitter and umami (meaty/savoury), and this influences the things that they love to eat; not surprisingly, primarily meaty flavours.

Each dog will have their preferences for taste and texture and so we should take the time to learn what they love most and care for least in order to maximize our success when using food rewards in training.

Touch

It's easy to forget about your dog's sense of touch and how this can impact on their response to training and contact with you. While age and some conditions will affect tactile sensitivity, most dogs have a well-developed sense of touch due to their skin being richly innervated with receptors that provide information about temperature, pain, movements and texture.

They also use information collected via their whiskers, or vibrissae, to guide them in their environment and to detect air movement. Although they seem like rough protective soles, your dog's paw pads are a means to detect important information via touch receptors. As a social animal, touch between group members is an important feature of their communication and relationships.

Your dog is capable of differentiating between objects or textures through their sense of touch. This benefits them when working on tasks such as object recognition and search and rescue. This is also utilized by dogs that have other sensory challenges such as blindness.

INTERNAL CHEMISTRY

While the intent of this book is not to go into huge detail about your dog's physiology and neurobiology, it is useful to know that internal chemistry influences your dog's responses to games and the world around them.

Dopamine

This neurotransmitter is making itself well known in the world of dog training as more people become aware of some of the complex chemistry underlying the behaviours we are working with. Dopamine is associated with the brain's reward circuitry and is therefore very important to most aspects of brain games with dogs. When your dog (or you, since your brain works in the same way) experiences a pleasurable event, the brain releases dopamine. This is involved in motivation, exploring, being curious, learning and interacting; all things we will want to encourage during our activities. Dopamine is also involved in strengthening the neural connections involved in learning new skills and is critical to the feeling of satisfaction or reward too. Activating the dopamine system can help to alleviate some fear and anxiety and therefore can be useful in boosting positive emotions.

Serotonin

Another chemical involved in the transmission of signals in the brain, this neurotransmitter is commonly associated with feelings of wellbeing and happiness. It has many roles including helping to regulate mood, social behaviour, appetite, sleep and memory. Levels of serotonin in the brain are therefore connected to mood, and low levels have been linked to aggression. Consistent and rewarding training and social interaction create positive emotions that in turn boost serotonin production, meaning that dogs that frequently engage in active, enjoyable training with you may be more resilient to the challenges linked to anxiety or stress.

Adrenaline (aka epinephrine)

This familiar hormone and neurotransmitter is involved in physiological and psychological responses to stress or arousal. In order to manage these during your sessions, it is important to understand that adrenaline can be both useful and detrimental to your dog.

Moderate levels will improve your dog's alertness and responsiveness, which will help them to engage in your training. It can also improve your dog's physical performance by increasing heart rate, blood flow and transportation of oxygen to the muscles where it is needed. This makes the dog faster, more powerful and enthusiastic.

The negative side of things is that, in excess, adrenaline will lead to overexcitement and more impulsive behavioural responses. It actually leads to a reduction in focus and therefore a loss of overall control. Adrenaline is also part of the body's natural fight-or-flight response, which is triggered when your dog perceives a threat. The outcome when this is triggered is that they may start to become distracted and concerned about the situation. High levels of adrenaline impair your dog's ability to focus, retain information and respond to your training cues. Therefore it is important to observe your dog and create breaks, or change the routine, if you see your dog becoming over-aroused.

Cortisol

Produced by the adrenal glands during times of physical or emotional stress or arousal, this hormone is designed to help the body cope with the experience. The difficulty is that if your dog is overexcited for too long, the levels of cortisol may become excessive and this can impair cognitive function and memory. Elevated levels have been shown to reduce the ability to focus, concentrate and learn, which clearly is a hindrance to your brain-training activities.

Limit the games of 'fetch'

It is becoming increasingly recognized that constant games of fetch are not ideal for your dog. This high-energy, exciting game can be fine in controlled situations, but many dogs love it so much that they will play on and on, eventually becoming addicted to the arousal it creates. The physical strain can be significant but the repeated release of adrenaline and cortisol can eventually lead to other problematic responses involving frustration and excessive agitation.

Many dogs can cope with controlled access to these highly exciting games and, as long as you schedule in breaks and more focused activities, they are likely to avoid problems. Some more sensitive dogs, and those that are naturally programmed to be easily aroused, might do better avoiding these sorts of games altogether.

WHAT CAN MY DOG REMEMBER?

Dogs possess both short-term and long-term memory, allowing them to recall events, people and locations over extended periods of time. They are also included in the species that display episodic-like memory, which means that they can recall specific past events and adapt their future behaviour based on this information. For example, if your dog had a wonderful experience during a particular walking adventure with you, they are able to recall the emotional associations with this experience when they are taken to new places, and this influences their responses, building anticipation and emotional changes based on past memory. Of course, this can work against them too with negative experiences.

Games and training rely on your dog building lasting associations with objects, activities and rules. Just like with people, some dogs have a better ability to 'remember' than others and, as mentioned previously, factors such as excitability and stress will impact on their ability to store information. In general, dogs tend to live for the moment rather than being bogged down by longer-term considerations. However, this is not indicative of a lack of intelligence; it's because their ultimate survival hasn't relied upon complex cognitive events in the way that humans' has.

Individual and breed differences will influence the success of any cognitive challenge but, if given routine and consistency, your dog is likely to be able to make connections and be capable of learning new games and actions. Research by scientists such as psychologist Stanley Coren has suggested that an average dog's brain and emotional capacity matures to that akin to a two-and-a half-year-old child. This research actually alludes to the dog's capacity to experience the emotional responses of joy, fear, anger, disgust and love, which are noted in children at roughly this age, as well as the fact that they do not develop responses such as shame, guilt, pride or contempt, which children do not display until between three and five years of age.

ALL DOGS ARE NOT THE SAME: KNOWING YOUR DOG

Several factors impact on how your dog responds to events around them. We understand that the combination of genetics and life experience during your dog's developmental stages creates a unique individual temperament with scope to respond to and learn from further events.

Puppies that have the opportunity to experience a wide range of events during the early stages of their life are more likely to develop resilience to stressors and to be confident, explorative individuals later on. Genetics influence how impulsive an individual might be and it is important to consider the selection pressures that have shaped your dog's breed lineage.

However, there is great variability in the behaviours depicted by members of any breed, no matter how many times we hear the statement: 'Oh that's a typical collie/ spaniel/terrier ...' While it may be possible to make generalizations, individuals within a breed are unique; expect to see a range of responses with some being more extreme than others. For example, within a population of scent hounds, most will have an interest and skill in detecting scents, some will be extremely sensitive and very keen to seek scents as often as they can, and a remaining portion will have lower interest and skill. This is absolutely normal and means that different breed groups are less distinct than we sometimes think.

Having said this, it is important to consider your dog's breed type since this helps you to understand what sorts of behaviours they are most likely to want to perform. Anticipate those behaviours and then learn what other activities they seek to perform by providing opportunities for them.

Domestication has altered our dog's brains. No longer needing to problem-solve to survive, our dogs have smaller relative brain size compared to wolves but more highly developed regions to process emotional and social behaviour. While research is still ongoing, structural differences between the brains of dogs from different breed groups has been reported. In remarkable studies, dogs were taught to lie still for MRI scans so that their brain activity and structure could be observed. We learned that dog brains have different developmental emphasis depending upon the area of specialism the breed was bred to possess. For example, scent hounds have additional dedicated areas to process odours.

Still dubious about the abilities of your little toy breed? These dogs have been selected over many generations to be smaller in size and are often kept as companions or 'lap dogs'. Many consider them to be less clever than their larger relations who still perform traditional roles.

But in fact, some research has shown that the brains of toy breeds have more capacity for perception, decision-making and problem-solving than some of the larger breeds! Though another study comparing absolute brain size found that smaller dog brains had less capacity for self-control and short-term memory. While they tend to have more sensitive arousal systems (which can be a positive or a negative), overall small dogs are often not given the credit they perhaps are due; by adapting our training routines they can be remarkable students.

GAMES AT DIFFERENT AGES

Throughout your dog's life and whenever you are considering what new activities to engage in with them, you must consider life stage and health factors. While your puppy is growing, it is important to protect their developing bones and joints from damage, so heavy physical exertion is best avoided. If your dog is an adult, but experiences pain from joints or other conditions, these should be explored with your veterinarian before you begin new activities. Remember that pain can lead to irritability and increased likelihood of behaviours that could be considered reactive and unacceptable. Any sudden behavioural changes should warrant a check-up by your veterinarian.

Breeds that have been selected to fulfil a particular role have unsurprisingly had their sensory system altered to improve their ability to do the job well. Scent hounds have increased olfactory receptors and sight hounds have altered visual processing. By considering the breed or breeds that have combined to create your dog, you might gain some insight into what they may be motivated to do. Having said this, every dog is unique and you might need to explore what your dog loves most. Observe them during different activities: what distracts them? What excites them? These clues will help you to discover your dog's favourite pastime.

SETTING THE FOUNDATIONS FOR GAMES AND TRAINING

Did you know that the process of learning is similar across species? While the information they can perceive and process might be different, learning via making an association between events and actions is a widespread response allowing animals to adapt to their environment.

A process called associative learning allows your dog to connect specific cues such as your verbal signal, or hand gesture, to a specific action or outcome. Our awareness of this allows us to manipulate the situation to ensure that our dogs connect the appropriate events together for training success.

Yes, admittedly we all have examples of our dogs connecting unintended things too. Perhaps your dog gets very excited and runs to the door when the adverts start during your regular TV show. It is likely that your dog has associated the action of being let out into the garden during this time and has connected the sound of the adverts starting as the cue. Other dogs might appear from all corners of the home when they hear the fridge door open, having connected this sound with the possibility of getting a corner of cheese if they look at you in just the right way. Associations are being made whether we mean them to be or not, so being aware of this can help you to maximize your success with training and to minimize the unwanted responses.

HOW DOES MY DOG LEARN?

We are all familiar with the concept of rewarding our dogs to encourage desirable behaviour. Consequences shape whether an action is repeated again or not. An action that results in a treat or some other pleasurable result is likely to be chosen again, whereas if that action results in something unpleasant, it becomes less likely to occur again. This basic principle forms the basis for your training with your dog.

'Reward your dog' sounds like such an easy concept. However, whether something is 'rewarding' is dependent upon the current state of your dog. If they have a full belly, a dry biscuit may not appeal; even the nicest treats become less desirable the more they are offered. We have probably all experienced this when we start with the first delicious chocolate or slice of cake, which, by the umpteenth serving, starts to feel a little less wonderful – there can be too much of a good thing.

Each individual is unique with their own preferences: you can get to know your dog and learn their favourites so you always have a way to encourage desirable responses. There are few things that can always be considered a reward, since it depends so much on your dog, how they feel at that moment, what they are motivated to do and so on. Get to know your dog, understand their favourite things and always have an array of options ready to use to strengthen desirable behaviours.

When we strengthen an action by rewarding it, we increase the dog's motivation to do it again and the likelihood that your dog will perform the action in the future with enthusiasm, be optimistic and open to further learning.

You don't need to be a professional dog trainer to benefit from an awareness of the learning terminology frequently used, sometimes wrongly, across all forms of media:

Positive Reinforcement	Positive Punishment	Negative Reinforcement	Negative Punishment
By adding something NICE, the target behaviour is strengthened.	By adding something UNPLEASANT, the target behaviour is weakened.	By removing something UNPLEASANT, the target behaviour is strengthened.	By removing something NICE, the target behaviour is weakened.
Emotional response: 'Yippee!'	Emotional response: 'Ouch!'	Emotional response: 'What a relief!'	Emotional response: 'Awww, I regret that.'
Think: treats, toys, pleasure of all sorts.	Think: smack, shout, pinch, pain and discomfort.	Think: removing pressure, threat or discomfort.	Think: removing the treat, toy or social contact.

There are lots of debates and varied ethical viewpoints regarding the training of dogs. In truth, a purely positive training world where everything is a 'yes' is not realistic, but it is possible and highly encouraged to engage with your dog in the most positive way possible, setting them up for success, giving clear instruction, encouragement and forming the strongest bond possible. Sometimes you might withhold attention or access to a treat while you wait for the right response to be presented, and for the majority of dogs this will not be traumatic or damaging to your relationship.

The reward savings account

It can help to visualize the rewards and fun things you do with your dog as though you are paying into their positive emotions savings account. If you have nicely invested with regular contributions, then the occasional negative blip that naturally comes along with life (such as having to administer medicine, or accidentally creating frustration during training) won't send your relationship with your dog into arrears.

Punishment, which includes all forms of interaction that your dog may find unpleasant (shouting, jerking, smacking and spraying), *might* carve you a path towards the desired response but may also leave many undesirable outcomes in its wake, such as increased anxiety or aggression. Behaviour that has been encouraged via punitive training will still occur, but never with as much enthusiasm as rewarded behaviour, and surely games and brain training are all about willing engagement between you and your dog. Ultimately, research does demonstrate that training through positive reinforcement has numerous benefits for both the dog and the human–animal bond alike, making it the welfare-friendly choice. Therefore, throughout this book you are going to be encouraged to use well-timed rewards and step-by-step approaches that will help your dog to succeed and to thoroughly enjoy themselves along the way.

WHAT IS THE BEST WAY TO TEACH MY DOG?

You will be presented with suggestions to teach the games in this book but there are always alternative ways to teach almost everything. It is important to consider your dog and to start with lessons that they are physically capable of. If they are not used to training, start small and build up their confidence and stamina over time. All individuals respond to rewards, though with some dogs you might have to work harder to discover what truly motivates them.

REWARDING YOUR DOG: NOT ALWAYS AS EASY AS IT SOUNDS

What reward to choose?

Choose what motivates your unique dog. This might be cheery praise, a friendly tickle or a treat; whatever your dog loves will be fine. Food is the most common reward for new and more challenging tasks since dogs are naturally driven to seek food and it automatically evokes pleasure. As you get to know your dog you might have to try a range of different food rewards before you understand which they like, which they love and which really gets their tail wagging. Having a range of options allows you to choose what to use for easier or more challenging training, and a bit of variety is great to keep them interested.

If your dog loves toys then you will have to understand what type of toy and what type of play really motivates them. They will have a preference and knowing this will empower you to keep them engaged. Try things out, watch your dog and learn from their responses.

It is easier to repeat several rounds of practice with treats than it is with a toy, since you will have to be prepared for your dog to engage with the toy to its satisfaction before removing it and resetting the training position to go again.

Food rewards should be small enough that you can use several within a training session; tiny fingernail-sized pieces are usually perfect. Be prepared to offer something larger (or more than one) if your dog presents an amazing response earlier than expected. Always be ready to encourage responses you want to see more of. Keep your treats in a pouch so that you can easily grab them when training (and to prevent your pockets from getting stained and being constantly full of forgotten morsels!).

Variety is interesting

Be prepared for your dog to change their mind. As with all cognitive beings, dogs have moods where they feel like doing something one day and are less inclined to do so the next. A reward can never be forced; if you're not in the mood for that particular slice of cake and someone forces it into your mouth, it doesn't make it any more tempting. Pushing a treat into your dog's mouth when they are focused elsewhere does not make it a rewarding experience, so be flexible and always have alternatives to work with if one reward becomes less interesting.

Observation and timing

You need to become very observant so that you can praise or reward your dog when they are actually performing the desired behaviour. Wait too long or look the other way and you will miss the moment, making it difficult to communicate to your dog that this was the response you want them to repeat in future. The best way to use your 'rewards' is to present them, or your marker signal (see page 41), as close to the desirable behaviour as possible. It can really help your timing to wear a treat pouch to allow ready access, or at least to have your clicker in hand to mark the desired behaviour instantly, and a treat pot nearby to provide the expected reward shortly after.

Make it relevant

If your dog's strongest motivation is to jump or chase, then you might struggle to convince them that a basic treat is of higher value. Sometimes you have to use the action your dog loves most as an incentive to strengthen other behaviours that you prefer. So, your dog wants to sniff the verge more than anything else? Use this as a reward for walking next to you on a loose lead for a few steps; one step, two steps and go sniff, etcetera. You can build up the desired behaviour and then release with permission to do the thing they love most.

Weight worries

If you are worried about your dog's weight, discuss this with your veterinarian. You do not need to add excessive additional calories to your dog's daily intake; instead you might consider reducing the size of main meals to allow for additional treats, or use the main meal itself during a training session and feed it piece by piece for successful responses. There are some healthier treats and even options for sensitive dogs. Most dogs can be rewarded in this manner with some creative thinking.

Regular reinforcement

There is a lot of science behind how often you should offer rewards during training sessions. However, the truth is that most of us aren't busy making mental calculations while multitasking or training our dogs to perform a particular action. Therefore the easiest routine is to reward continuously at first for every successful outcome while you set the scene and get your dog into the swing of the task, and then to move to a more random routine. This means that you either vary how many responses you require from your dog before you proffer the reward, or you get it to sustain an action for variable amounts of time. You can carefully increase the number of or duration of responses before the reward is offered to keep the skill progressing.

Is using treats just bribing?

Lots of canine carers are worried about the potential problems that may arise from using food rewards. It is sometimes considered to be bribing or 'cheating'. However, if you use the reward correctly you should not have to worry about this. Bribing is when you offer something to your dog to entice them to do what you want (usually to come to you, or to move in some way). Rewarding is different in that it comes after the behaviour has occurred, as a form of payment. There is a big difference in these options with regards to developing reliable responses and it is unwise to develop the habit of bribing or luring your dog too often. While luring is a useful starting point for many lessons, it should be phased out as early as possible to prevent problems.

Other owners worry that they will be stuck using

rewards forever. In fact, with good training you should be able to motivate your dog to build up their response over time so that they are happy to do more to earn the reward. You will notice that in the early stages of most games you will have to use frequent rewards to kick-start the concept. As the skill grows and the game itself becomes rewarding, the frequency of treats can be reduced. Throughout the games in this book you will be advised to use some treats, or your dog's main food, to get the games started.

Want to stop rewarding entirely? Your clever dog will choose activities that feel pleasurable for them, and while many games are enjoyable in their own right, others require more concentration and self-control and are likely to become less fun to your dog if they never receive sufficient reinforcement for performing them. How would you respond if your boss declared that now you are good at your job they don't feel the need to pay you any longer? Scientific research has shown that when reinforcement stops, actions that previously resulted in a reward start to diminish and the animal will start to seek out other more reliable ways to receive rewards. Ask yourself why you would want to stop rewarding your clever dog for doing smart behaviours when they could easily be choosing wilder, less appropriate activities. It is absolutely okay to continue to praise, pet and treat your dog for being amazing.

WHAT IS CLICKER TRAINING AND DO I NEED TO DO IT?

Clicker training is a popular method to use when teaching animals to perform new actions. The 'clicker' is the name for a small plastic gadget with a metal tongue that makes a 'click' when pressed. This sound has no meaning to your dog before training commences, but through a process called classical conditioning (where the 'click' is paired with a reward) it comes to have meaning and to be a useful training tool. Once your dog has an automatic response to the click, i.e. they respond by looking for the expected treat, it can be used as a signal of reward to indicate the occurrence of 'correct' behaviours so that your dog repeats those again.

Marker signals

It is important to have a way to 'mark' actions that you would like to see more of even if you are not able to immediately reward your dog with a treat or toy in that situation. For example, your dog (who is 20 metres away from you) looks at, but chooses to ignore, the remains of someone's sandwich on the ground. You want to reward that choice there and then, but by the time you walk over to your dog, or call them away, time will have passed and they may be thinking of something else when you pull a treat from your pouch, making the association rather ambiguous. Instead, having a way to 'mark' the good decision – in this case, the turning away from a potential snack – is vital. You could instead 'click' or use a marker word such as 'yes' or 'good' to communicate with your dog that their choice was great and that a reward will be on its way shortly.

The closer this signal or mark is to the desired behaviour, the more likely it is to have the impact you want. The treat can then follow afterwards, but the emotional response of anticipating and receiving the reward will still be associated with the behaviour that was occurring when the click or signal occurred. Throughout the games in this book you will be encouraged to use a marker signal of your choice.

'All done' can be a useful cue that tells your dog that the activity is over and they can move away. Use the same cue each time on the completion of any task or game.

DOES A CLICKER SUIT MY TRAINING?

When deciding whether to use a clicker or not you should consider your routine, your dog's experiences and temperament. Some dogs are scared of the sound, some owners have enough on their hands and don't want another thing to remember. In the end, training has to suit you and your dog so choose the method that works best for you.

The marker signal you choose can be a click, or a well-timed verbal signal (such as 'yes', 'yup', 'good', 'nice'). Any sound can be paired with a reward and therefore primed to have meaning. The best response comes from novel sounds, so if you usually do a lot of talking to your dog you need to think of a word that you don't often or ever use and say it in a way that emphasizes its importance. Alternatively, you can create a clicking sound with your tongue, which can also be effective.

Introducing a clicker

When you first begin using it, the clicker will have no meaning at all for your dog so your first task is to create the desired association. This part is sometimes called 'tuning' or 'charging' your clicker and involves tossing a treat to the floor, or offering it from your hand, and at the exact moment they go to eat it, click the clicker. The repetition of the click–treat experience begins to build neural connections between the two things and soon your dog will anticipate the arrival of a treat when they hear the click.

The click now means: 'Yes! A treat is on its way!' This naturally creates positive expectations for your dog when they hear that sound.

Now, while clicker training is a positive way of training, it is important to follow some basic rules to ensure that it works well for you:

. . . .

Once the association is established, you should only click when you see desirable actions. Don't be tempted to click just to get their attention.

The click needs to predict the arrival of a reward, so be ready to follow up with a treat shortly afterwards. Too many clicks without reinforcement and your dog will start to be less interested, as the signal is no longer reliable.

If your dog flinches, cringes, moves away or shows other signs that they are uncomfortable with the clicker, you should stop and consider whether this is the best option for your dog. Some sensitive dogs can cope with quieter models of clickers, or where the sound is muffled by being held in your hand, up a sleeve and behind your back. Adapt to suit your dog and remember that you can use the clicker concept with a marker word instead, with great results.

. . . .

HOW MUCH TRAINING SHOULD I DO?

There is no set answer for this since we all have different dogs and routines. Puppies will have shorter attention spans and more need for rest than an average adult dog. Elderly dogs will tire more easily and possibly feel less motivated than younger dogs. Breed differences and health challenges will all influence how much activity they will enjoy. Expect to have a gradual change in activity from puppy through to the elderly stages of life. Remain mindful of current changes such as the weather or household routines as these may cause patterns of activity to change too.

One startling realization for many owners is that since your dog is always learning, every moment is a learning opportunity. As no one can, or wants to, actively train 24/7, the ideal situation is to set your dog up for success by minimizing the opportunity to make mistakes or to do things we would prefer they didn't.

TIME BUDGETS

We are very familiar with how a busy routine can impact on the time available for hobbies and entertainment. However, when you have a dog there is more to consider than just the time it might take to walk them each day. Every dog has unique needs, but in general it is useful to consider how they spend their time. It is not healthy for a dog to be active all day long; this is a recipe for over-arousal and associated problems. Some dogs are naturally busier than others, but as a general rule, aim for 20 per cent of your dog's day to involve some form of physical activity (walking, training, playing with others or by themselves). Before you rush off to do some detailed calculations, it is useful, typically, to set aside around 30 minutes a day at a minimum for deliberately planned brain training (which can be broken into shorter sessions to suit). Walks and other active time should be in addition to this.

WHY DOESN'T MY DOG SEEM EASY TO TRAIN?

There will always be different styles of learners among our dogs. Some breeds have been selected to be strongly motivated to respond to their handler's signals; others, to be independent and more interested in following scents or chasing prey. Your unique dog has their own learning style that you can get to know over time.

The hard truth is that often when our dogs are not picking up on a lesson, it is because we are failing to be as clear as we should be and they don't understand what they are meant to be learning. So don't get frustrated. Stop, step back and consider if you could make the steps easier for your dog, reduce distractions, reward in a more timely manner, use nicer rewards and so on. During training it's not just your dog that is learning new skills – you are, too, and you will be constantly improving your observation and motor skills as you practise.

If your dog is anxious or fearful, this will impact on their ability to learn and to focus on the training. It would be sensible then to address the negative emotions or choose a different, more comforting location to train in, or a game that they feel more comfortable with. Your veterinarian will be able to guide you to an appropriately qualified specialist to help you with whatever problem you are facing.

IS MY DOG ENJOYING THE GAME?

While the intention behind all of the suggestions in this book is to promote positive wellbeing for our dogs, not all will enjoy every activity. If your dog is of a more sensitive nature they may not have the confidence to play wherever and whenever. New activities and objects should be introduced slowly and your dog given time to explore and become familiar before they have to do specific tasks.

Some dogs are easily startled, and overenthusiastic praise or celebratory movements by their handler can put them off playing further. Some are wary of being reached over or having certain areas touched. Be mindful of your dog's preferences when you choose which game to play. Take things slowly and remember that games are meant to be participated in willingly, otherwise the fun is lost.

Some readers will own rescue dogs that had a previous life elsewhere, perhaps where they did not learn to play or engage with toys. These will need time to settle in and to be coaxed gently and carefully into learning some play skills. Sadly, if an adult dog has never had the opportunity to play they may never learn all the usual skills, but it is always worth patiently exploring games to see what they seem to like, and then helping them to learn by playing little and often. If they have never had to use their brain in mental tasks this might also be an initial hurdle. Slow down and adjust your expectations; there is no absolute end goal for many games and we should celebrate all the small wins with our dogs.

Not all the games in this book will suit all dogs.

That would be an impossible task with the wide range of personalities and skills out there. However, most can be adapted in some form. Always use your own knowledge of your dog and their habits to keep them safe. For example, if your dog is a known scavenger and consumer of non-food items then please be careful with cardboard, paper and other materials that could be ingested. While these are usually safe if the dog is supervised, since the aim of the games is to benefit you and your dog's relationship, it's important to avoid any chance of foreign body ingestion while playing. Always choose toys and tools appropriate in size and strength for your dog.

Throughout all training please pay attention to your dog: are they tired, hot, cold, thirsty, worried, confused or experiencing another feeling that might distract from their learning? Aim for comfort and take plenty of breaks to account for their needs.

BODY LANGUAGE TO BE AWARE OF

Although humans and dogs have cohabited for such a long time, we remain fairly poor at reading some of their communication signals unless we practise doing so. Studies have shown that, in general, whether we live with a dog or not, humans are good at recognizing the extreme signals of anger, fear and happiness in dogs. However, the myriad subtle signs that occur before the extreme emotions develop are less well understood, meaning that important responses are missed. Adults are better at reading dogs than children are, but the results are fairly poor overall. If we were more tuned in we could detect when our dogs start to feel concern, or struggle in other ways. Think how happy your dog will be when they find communicating with you has become easier.

Being aware of the overall meaning of canine signalling and combining this with knowledge of your unique dog is important. Their individual behaviour pattern and personality will shine through and it is important to observe your dog in a range of situations to fully understand their responses and learn to notice the more subtle signs.

Some of the important aspects of canine signalling to look out for include:

Whole body

Dogs communicate with their whole body so it is important to look out for as many signals as you can in order to interpret the meaning properly. Looking at just the tail or the mouth will only give you part of the story.

Tail

Let's start with the tail: this acts like a flag, sending information from a distance. The biggest mistake we make with tails is the belief that a wagging tail equals a happy dog. This is untrue. In fact, wagging signals arousal, which is not always a positive emotion. Look at the position and the tension in the tail to tell you more. Held high and stiff indicates alertness and sometimes accompanies aggression. The lower the tail is held, the more fear or submission the dog intends to convey. Slow wagging is more tentative, while an enthusiastic wag involving the whole bottom area is certainly a positive signal.

Ears

Depending on your dog's physical morphology, or shape, ears may not always be easy to read. Even with those having long, hairy ears, though, you can look for clues. The base of the ear moves and can be used to interpret mood changes. Forward-facing is generally an indication of interest or alertness; something you want to see while your dog is playing or training with you. If the ears are pulled back to flatten against the head, this indicates a negative emotion such as fear or anxiety. Sideways-facing ears can be a signal of no-threat or appeasement and might indicate they are unsure during a game.

Eyes

Where and how your dog 'looks' can communicate a great deal. If they are relaxed and comfortable, your dog's eyes should appear soft rather than surrounded by tense muscles. A hard stare, where the dog is intensely fixated on the target, accompanied by tight muscles and forward movement or weight shift, is likely to indicate a threatening intent. In a fearful dog it is typical to see the face and head muscles pull taught (moving the ears back and opening the eyes wider), which results in the whites (sclera) of the eyes showing. This crescent of white, which is not seen in most relaxed dogs, is sometimes called mood-eye or whale-eye, and is considered to be a sign of emotional discomfort.

Mouth

While we pay a lot of attention to bared teeth, we often forget to consider our dog's mouth the rest of the time. If your dog is relaxed, they will generally have a slightly open mouth and possibly be panting lightly. Closing their mouth might indicate they are focusing, perhaps on the game you are playing, but this can also occur prior to a more aggressive response. If you notice the tongue-tip briefly flick out towards the nose, this may be indicative of social concern, anxiety or fear, and should not be dismissed as just an appreciation of treats.

Yawning can sometimes indicate tiredness, but unless your dog has just woken up, it is more likely to be an effort to signal feelings of stress. This might be your dog's way of trying to relax you; perhaps you are tense while trying to teach them a new game. It may be their way of signalling that they are confused about what they are meant to be doing. If you think this might be the case, stop, take a break to dismiss any tension, and come back fresh and enthusiastic in a while.

Teeth on display

Hopefully your dog will enjoy the games you play, but sometimes situations occur where a dog feels that they have to communicate with a strong display, including a snarl to expose the teeth. If the front canines are on show, along with a direct stare, this is a significant message. Stop what you are doing, give your dog space and time to settle. Think carefully about what was going on leading up to this incident, since it is very unlikely it came from nowhere.

Other dogs present with what is termed a 'submissive' grin. In this posture, dogs will pull their lips back to show almost all of their teeth while squinting their eyes, and probably pulling their ears to the side or backwards. This can be seen during social greetings or if the dog is feeling uncomfortable with your behaviour and is trying to appease you. In that case, stop, give them some space and think about whether you are pushing the games or interaction a bit too hard.

Hair movement

Again, we often ignore changes in our dog's coats. However, if you see the hair along the centre of your dog's back – the hackles – rising (also called pilo-erection), this indicates that arousal levels are rising. This is not necessarily a negative response, but consider other signs too before deciding.

Body posture

Some of the games will encourage a variety of postures, but be mindful of your dog's natural posture in between sessions. If they feel relaxed, your dog will have their weight distributed evenly. A worried dog will have a lowered posture, or their weight shifted away from the 'scary' thing. If your dog is positioning themself very low to the ground or rolling over onto their back, this is a sign of real discomfort and it should *not* be interpreted as a request for a belly-rub. The fear roll-over looks very different to a happy belly-rub invitation, which includes more wagging, fewer other signs of tension, and is likely to involve more movement and excitement overall.

Hopefully you will see lots of play signalling while you are with your dog. Play-bowing, with chest low to the ground and raised bottom, is a key indication that they are engaging with the right mindset.

PANDEMIC PUPPIES

The impact of the Covid-19 pandemic on our companion canines has been significant. Professional reports from veterinarians, behaviourists, trainers and groomers have indicated that dogs have been affected in several ways that may be important to consider when deciding to train them for any new activity, even games.

Many puppies raised and homed during the lockdown stages of the pandemic are finding it challenging to socialize with new people and dogs, and may be less confident when faced with novelty or difficult problems. While research is still underway, this appears to be in part due to the necessary limitations placed on the extent to which breeders and owners could socialize them during the animals' formative first months and through their first year of life. Litters of puppies probably had fewer visitors, if any, and contact with new people was typically done from a distance, or with the puppy away from their owner who would normally provide social support. Many people recall the feelings of worry and concern we experienced during this time, which has undoubtedly influenced our choices with our pets too. Training classes were either cancelled or held online, which did open opportunities for owner–dog interaction but did not broaden the dog's worldliness. These experiences have impacted on the confidence and robustness of many dogs. They are still beloved pets, but support and training aimed at rectifying behavioural difficulties is currently in very high demand.

Many dogs were rescued from animal shelters during the lockdowns. These will have a range of backgrounds and life experiences, meaning they have different skills and interests in people and training. There is no reliable rule to predict behaviour as it is a culmination of genetics and life experiences together, and each individual is unique.

Adult dogs who remained in their own homes during the pandemic were also influenced by the sudden lifestyle changes we experienced. Owners were often home all the time and this led to increased attachment, where dogs became accustomed to constant company. Other dogs found it stressful to have their family home all day and developed behavioural changes because they no longer had their usual routine. Exercise was curtailed for many, play dates and group walks were not possible, which affected their overall social ability. Many dogs did not attend regular veterinary visits due to access restrictions and therefore may not have had health problems recognized. The sudden return to work of many owners has been a shock to their pets, many of whom are now feeling anxious, struggling with long periods alone. Overall, no group of dogs went unaffected by the necessary lockdown events and the impact is likely to be noticeable for some time to come.

Playing games with your dog is a wonderful way to bond and to build a strong relationship. However, there are some circumstances that might cause your dog to struggle. You might be seeking new games in order to resolve or relieve some of the resulting challenges from the pandemic. Be mindful about the needs of your individual dog, taking the time needed to learn the basics, hone your own training skills to minimize human errors, and most of all, be patient. Allow them time to become accustomed to new items, particularly those that are noisy or may move suddenly. Allow for repetition and ensure that you reward all achievements. Dogs that are feeling anxious may learn at a slower rate and struggle more with problem-solving, so you might have to adjust your expectations. Choosing options that suit the nature and capabilities of your dog will help them to gain confidence; all dogs should be able to learn and enjoy several of the games described in this book, albeit with your own modifications and changes. Games should be fun for all, so relax and enjoy the experience with your dog, no matter whether they perfect it or not.

TIPS FOR WORKING WITH LESS CONFIDENT DOGS

- Find a place to train where your dog feels safe and secure. Minimize distractions.

- If they are worried by other pets, train them alone. If they find confidence from being around other dogs, allow them to watch you training them first, then give the opportunity for them to have a go.

- Keep the games brief and start with simple steps that are easy to achieve. Frequent rewards will help to build confidence.

- Stay calm and patient and take a break if you feel frustrated.

- End the game while your dog is still keen so that they are enthusiastic when you offer the chance to play again.

ARE YOU READY TO GET STARTED?

Keeping your dog's mind busy helps to hone their natural skills, keeping them mentally stimulated, enriched and satisfied. Without this, their innate instincts and need to express natural behaviour might find an outlet in less desirable behaviours such as foraging in your bin or chewing on your favourite shoes.

As opposed to physical activities, where both you and your dog need to be able to run, jump and perform, many brain-training options are suitable for dogs and owners of all ages and abilities.

The range of options for brain training and enrichment is endless. All of your dog's natural senses should be stimulated, and by engaging in different activities it is possible for you to bring these opportunities into their routine. Depending on your dog's natural abilities, they will be more skilled in certain areas. This is part of the bonus gained from engaging in these activities; you find out what your dog's 'superpowers' are. Will they be an avid scent detector, or skilled at reading visual cues? Will they be perfectly able to shut out distractions and focus on a task? Let's find out.

EQUIPMENT

This is a list of the items most commonly called for in the exercises that follow.

Bin or basket: This can be used to drop items into, as platforms to step on or to hide things behind.

Card squares and marker pens: The size should allow you to create clear visual signs for your dog to follow.

Cardboard boxes: Various sizes of box (free from staples) can be used in play. The paper packing material that comes with certain purchases can also be used (see page 97).

Clicker: Many styles of clicker exist but the important aspect is that the sound is clear and you are able to easily press the tongue to create the 'click' sound. This might mean having it on a lanyard or wristband for easy access.

Cushion: A small cushion prop is useful for different activities (and can be kneeled on for games that require you to be down at your dog's level for a while).

DIY agility options: You might use purpose-bought items, but you can create some great activities using broom handles, benches, tables, chairs, footstools, buckets, garden canes, draped towels or blankets. Options depend on the area you are in and the size of your dog. Always consider risk of damage and injury.

Dog food: Some activities call for use of a portion of your dog's regular daily meal.

Dog-specific items: There are items that we use for day-to-day training that can be useful in more complex games too.

Electronic button or bells: You might want to purchase a set of buttons with the option to record your voice instructions. A set of hanging bells can also be used if preferred.

Household items: There are many useful items you might have at home. Always check for risks and consider alternatives if there is danger of damage or if they are made from delicate material.

Human items: Items that were never intended to be playthings can be useful as educational props. These might include an old glove, shoe or a broken remote (no batteries).

Lead: Your dog's regular lead can be used in play, or just to keep them safe.

Muffin tray: A simple baking tray with spaces for six muffins works perfectly.

Nail file board: To make your own nail board you will need a solid board that is of sufficient size to suit your dog. For small to medium dogs you could use a chopping board, while larger dogs will probably need a length of plywood board. One-hundred-grit sandpaper sheets, glued on, or anti-slip safety walk tape work well. An alternative option is to use a length of plastic piping cut in half, with the sandpaper sheets glued into the centre. This may provide more contact for the side nails but will require more precision than a flat board due to the smaller area.

Plastic cones: Depending on the size of your dog and the likelihood of them picking up and playing with the cone, you can opt for children's or full-sized cones such as those used in several sports activities.

Plastic cups, tubs or bowls: Opaque cups (at least three) to hide treats underneath.

Plates: You can use paper or plastic plates. If using breakable options, please take care.

Recycle and play: Many items such as empty plastic bottles can be reused as props to play with. Old towels can be knotted up as pullies or toys.

Rug or mat: It is sometimes recommended that your dog lies on a soft surface during a game. Rather than using their own bed, it is often easier to use a small rug or mat, which can be moved to accommodate the game or lifted between games.

Stacking cups: Toddler toys, or used paper cups, or small boxes can be used to create a tumbling tower game (see page 250).

Sticky notes: Spare sticky notes or Washi tape can be useful for some of the target marker games.

String: You will need two or three 30- to 50-centimetre lengths. Hessian jute string, ribbon or other rope will do.

Towel: A towel suitable for the size of your dog is ideal. Preferably one that can be dedicated to their use.

Toy-box: This should be able to fit a range of toys but be easily accessible to your dog.

Toys: There are several games that will utilize your dog's toys. Ideally, have a selection of shapes and materials. They should be things your dog likes to play with but does not guard or become overexcited by. Suggestions included in this book are balls, lick mats, raggers, snuffle mats, a range of food dispensing toys, ball on a rope, flirt pole.

Treat pot: A container in which to keep your training treats is essential. You will need easy access to these while keeping them sufficiently contained that they do not distract your dog as they are learning.

Treat pouch: For the more active games you may want to wear a treat pouch so that you can quickly access the rewards without having to run back to your treat pot elsewhere. A pouch saves your pockets from nuisance crumbs and staining.

Treats: You will see frequent mention of this throughout the game instructions. What you use will depend upon your dog and their own preferences. In most cases small treats will work well, though you can mix up different food options to create treats of differing value.

Yoga ball: Smaller dogs can use a smaller plastic ball, but a yoga ball can be used for 'Ball skills' (page 109) or as part of other training such as in your 'Agility', 'Copy me', or 'Go around' lessons.

Yoga mat: This can be useful for sitting on as well as specifically for canine yoga games.

CHAPTER 1

START WITH THE BASICS

While the games discussed here are broken down into small parts to help you to succeed, there are a few common foundational skills that your dog should know and that will support many of the more complex games.

SIT

Many dogs know this cue, but if you are new to training you might not have covered it yet. It is a useful foundation for numerous games. Although it is commonly used for a range of circumstances, always consider whether it is appropriate for your dog to sit in the context in which you are asking. For example, if they are feeling uncomfortable near other dogs or 'scary' situations, this might not be the appropriate response for them. It is also important to consider how comfortable sitting is for older dogs or those with known orthopaedic problems.

WHAT YOU'LL NEED
- Some small treats to encourage the action

Get ready

While this is a fairly simple lesson that can be taught to the youngest of puppies, it is helpful to start in a quiet and comfortable location. Your dog may be happier to sit on a mat or carpet initially; wet grass is often off-putting!

Get steady

Make sure you have your dog's attention before your start.

Let's play!

Now take your treat in one hand and hold it close to your dog's nose, slowly moving it upwards and slightly back towards their body. As their nose rises their natural response is to lower their hindquarters and sit. As soon as their bottom touches the floor you should release the treat.

Practise a few times and start to say your cue word, 'sit', as they move into position. Make sure that you praise and reward all correct responses.

Once they can move into position easily, start to reduce the lure and make your hand signal smaller. A small upwards flick of the hand can become your cue, or you may rely entirely on the verbal cue if you wish.

TOP TRAINING TIPS

🐾 Focus on accuracy in your timing so that you are rewarding your dog for placing their bottom on the floor. If you wait too long they may raise a paw, or even start jumping up or mouthing on your hand. Resist repeating the cue 'sit, sit, sit'; be patient and wait for the correct response so you don't accidentally accustom your dog to respond to the repetition.

🐾 Once your dog is reliably sitting on cue, build up the level of difficulty by practising in different locations with more distractions. Shuffle your feet, jump, spin, raise your arms; if your dog can remain in position then they are a pro!

LIE DOWN

Get ready

Choose a quiet area with fewer distractions to begin. Get your dog's attention and encourage them to come close to you. If you have a very small dog you will need to start by sitting or crouching beside them.

Get steady

If you can encourage your dog into a 'sit' position first, the 'down' comes more easily.

Let's play!

Hold a treat close to your dog's nose and slowly lower it downwards, aiming for the area between their paws. In order to follow the treat your dog will bend their neck and lower their body to make it easier for them to remain close to the food. As soon as they move into a 'down' position be ready to release the treat and praise them.

Reset the position by encouraging them to get up again; possibly by tossing another treat a short distance away so they have to move to eat it.

Repeat the process and you will find that your dog gets faster at moving down. Take care to ensure that you release the treat when your dog is flat on the floor so that the lesson is clear for them.

Begin to add in your verbal cue of choice, 'down' or 'flat', just as your dog moves into the right position. If you automatically call 'down' when your dog jumps up or is on the furniture, then pick something else to use to mean lying on the floor. Repeat until they associate the cue with the action.

Fade out your treat lure by following the same action but without a treat in your hand. Once this is successful you can start to make your gesture less and less exaggerated so that you are no longer moving your hand all the way to the floor. Eventually, the signal will be a small gesture towards the floor.

TOP TRAINING TIPS

🐾 Very small dogs can sometimes take longer to lie down to follow the treat because they are already so close to the floor. Therefore, those with small breeds (dachshunds come to mind) might need to start very patiently. Try sitting on the floor with your legs outstretched in front of you. Bend a knee so that there is a small gap between the floor and your leg. Now lure your dog through this area by guiding with a treat in your hand; you'll find that they go down in order to follow the treat under your knee. The moment they do be ready to praise and reward them. Once they get the hang of it you can go back to regular techniques.

🐾 Bring on the challenge! Your dog will need to practise lying down despite various distractions and for different lengths of time before you expect them to be able to do this reliably when you take them to a café or expect them to sit for prolonged periods.

TAKE IT AND DROP

This combined lesson is something we can use on a daily basis with our dogs, in training, play and regular routine. It's very useful to teach our dogs this as early as possible, but it can be worked on at any stage in their lives. If your dog is presenting with signs of guarding behaviour please seek advice, since additional pressure to leave an item can create further problems; it is vital to approach this safely.

WHAT YOU'LL NEED
- A toy that your dog is interested in, but not one they are obsessed with

Get ready

Begin in a low-distraction environment. Have the toy and some treats available. Ideally, keep the treats in a pouch tucked behind you so that your dog is not distracted by them.

Get steady

Get your dog's attention and engage them with the toy – wiggle it, encourage them to grab it with their mouth. You want them to be playful but not wildly enthusiastic.

Let's play!

While playing with the toy in one hand, bring the other, holding a treat, close to their nose. Try to stop moving the toy if you can. Most dogs will let the toy go to eat the treat, at which point you can say your cue word 'drop'.

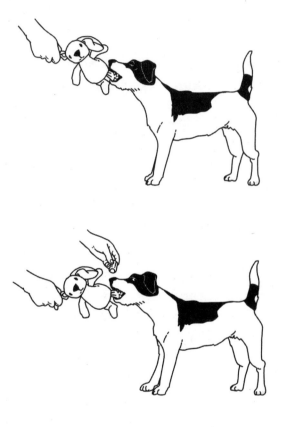

With practice you will be able to stop holding the treat to your dog's nose when asking them to 'drop'. When they do let go, praise them, offer a treat from your pouch and then resume.

Restart the game by offering the toy again and saying 'take it'. Practise by continuing the game and adding in 'drop' cues paired periodically with food. Give your 'drop' cue, wait for them to let go and them immediately praise and treat.

TOP TRAINING TIPS

🐾 Say your cues in a happy tone rather than sounding cross or confrontational. Remember that this is a game and if your dog sees this as a fun game they should always be happy to respond in a relaxed manner.

🐾 Start to wait for your dog to look at you briefly before you give your 'take it' cue again.

🐾 Work this lesson to include longer-lasting treats. To increase the challenge go slowly and make sure that letting go is highly rewarding.

HITTING THE MARK

Target training is a method used to encourage your dog to use different parts of their body to make contact with a specific target item: this might be a hand, a target stick, target marker or an object. Moving towards or positioning to touch this target is then reinforced to build towards the desired action.

Get ready

Choose your target. This depends on what you want to teach your dog to do. Active movement might be easier to encourage if your dog is moving towards your hand or a target stick. Focused tasks where you want your dog to remain in a static position, or where you want them to push on something, tend to find a fixed item useful: a sticky note, coloured tape or mat.

Usually the target is presented and your dog allowed to explore in their own time. It is important that they are comfortable with it, and you can start to build positive associations with their exploration by rewarding them for approaching, sniffing and touching it.

What action does targeting involve? Any body part can be used to make contact with the target but commonly the nose, paw and chin are used. If your dog is new to target training, or you are working through some of the games in this book, focus on one type of target touch at a time so that they don't get mixed up.

Get steady

Mark the behaviour. As with all the training in this book, your aim is to identify the moment your dog performs the desired behaviour and to reward it. This might be via a click (see clicker training, page 41) or via a verbal marker such as 'yes' to indicate to your dog that the action they are doing there and then is going to bring a reward their way. With targeting, the marker is given the moment your dog makes contact with the target, and over a series of repetitions this creates a connection between the action and the pleasure of receiving reinforcement. Once this occurs your dog will want to go and make contact again and again.

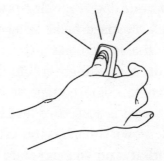

Once the contact is occurring reliably, you then work towards shaping the final desired behaviour. This might involve rewarding a brief pawing action initially, then a brief touch, then rewarding for contact held for a moment longer, prolonging the paw touch. Over time this may lead to the paw being held in place for the duration of the activity. Whatever you aim to teach, the gradual progression from an initial simple criterion to more complex criteria aims to move you towards your final action.

Finally, the target can be faded out, leaving the action itself, or the action can be generalized to occur in more contexts when the dog is cued. This means they can perform the action in different environments from where the initial learning occurred.

Let's play!
Hand target

A simple lesson that can extend to many different training contexts is a hand touch with the nose. This is easy to start with, since most dogs are comfortable approaching their owners and you don't require any tools.

Begin with your dog in front of you. Hold a treat on your palm, secured by your thumb. Hold it out and wait while your dog approaches it. The moment they make contact, give your marker signal, e.g. a click, and release the treat. Repeat a couple of times then move to different positions; slightly lower, slightly higher.

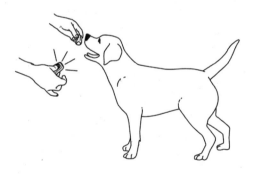

Add in your verbal cue, 'touch', just as your dog moves to make contact with your hand. Repeat this process so that it is connected with the action.

Increase your dog's enthusiasm to come forwards and touch by holding your hand out while stepping backwards and saying 'touch'. The contact should always result in the reward being offered.

Now that your dog is confident in the touch you can stop holding a treat in your hand, instead presenting the flat hand for them to approach and explore. They will anticipate the reward and will come and touch your hand with their nose as usual, at which point you should say 'touch' and throw a treat with your other hand onto the floor for your dog to move away to eat.

Moving them away from you allows you to reset, ready for another repetition of the training when they turn back to you.

Paw target

Some games require your dog to use their paw to make contact with an object. Individual differences will mean your dog may be more, or less, paw-focused when you start, but most can learn this action if given time and reinforcement.

Choose an appropriate marker: a plastic lid, a sticky note, a square of material etc. Encourage your dog to investigate and increase the likelihood of them using their paw on it by placing a treat underneath. Mark the exact

moment they use their paw and hopefully this contact will be captured so they are keen to repeat it. Advance the training in a similar manner to the hand-target strategy by practising in different places, sending your dog further to touch the target and by using a consistent verbal cue, e.g. 'press'.

TOP TRAINING TIPS

🐾 You might find that your dog tries to nudge your hand between training sessions. You can ignore this since the only time the treat is available is when the verbal cue 'touch' has occurred.

🐾 If your dog is opening their mouth instead of pressing with their nose, this is probably because your click or marker has been coming a little too late. Try to mark just as the nose contact occurs and not while they are already eating the treat. Changing strategy away from holding the treat in the targeted hand is often useful to change this response.

🐾 With the paw touch, pay attention to getting your timing precise when capturing the action or you might reinforce a scraping action instead; this might be useful for some games but not all.

🐾 Bring on the challenge! Present your hand while in new locations with a range of distractions about you. You might find that you have to work up to using it around the most exciting distractions, but this can be your personal challenge.

CHAPTER 2

LET'S BE HAPPY

Whether you are human or canine, having activities that occupy, challenge and develop us can benefit our emotional wellbeing. A feeling of accomplishment comes with succeeding in a new skill or task. This supports confidence growth and the development of a positive attitude. In addition to the known benefits that come from physical activity, research shows that keeping the brain active provides a positive impact on its overall health too.

As you will see, some of these games are about giving your dog agency over their actions. When you consider that most decisions in their lives are heavily controlled by our preferences, we can start to see how this can be an emotionally positive experience for the dog.

EXPLORATORY FREE PLAY

We can use the following as enrichment, as a way of regulating arousal levels or confidence building, depending on your dog's needs. The choices your dog makes are entirely their own. This game is based on the wonderful work of UK trainer Sarah Fisher, who utilizes 'ACE Freework' into her physical and behavioural assessments, but it can be a beneficial part of any dog's routine.

WHAT YOU'LL NEED

- A variety of different treats: small soft treats of different flavours, meat/cheese paste, kibble etc.
- A combination of the following, depending on what you have available:
  - Cardboard boxes of different sizes
  - Lick mats, plastic trays, other suitable surfaces for soft food to be pasted on
  - Snuffle mat, plastic cones
  - Raised platforms: kitchen step, plastic box
  - Carpet square, rubber matting/yoga mat, reflective foil blankets, bubble wrap
  - Dog activity toys
  - Box with paper packing material
  - Let your imagination go with this activity – any dog-safe item from the cupboard, shed or garage can be utilized!

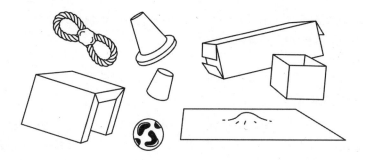

Get ready

Choose a selection of items you wish to use in today's set-up. While the choice will depend on the space you have available, starting with at least six different items will give a range of choices for your dog to explore.

Get steady

Set out your chosen items with sufficient space so that your dog can move easily between them and has to make choices about which they move towards. Set up options such as soft food on low and raised surfaces, treats on the floor and treats inside boxes or puzzle toys. In essence you are combining different levels of effort with a variety of movements. In between the food

options you can lay out different surfaces and obstacles to step over or around.

Let's play!

Let your dog in to explore this new set-up. Stand back and observe, allowing them time to explore and to decide what they want to go for first. This game is all about your dog choosing how they move and what they spend their time on.

Practise your observation skills: what does your dog home in on first? Do they tend to prefer things to their right or left? Do they select things that are at nose level, or items they can stretch down or up towards? What activities get their tail wagging and keep their attention for the longest? These are all valuable pieces of information to help you to understand your dog and any issues they may have.

TOP TRAINING TIPS

🐾 This is a great activity to help your dog to regulate their emotions after a stressful walk, or an activity where they have become overexcited.

🐾 Each time you set up this free play exercise you can vary the way it is organized.

🐾 Bring on the challenge! If your dog is very confident and eagerly moves through all the activities easily, then start to increase the complexity of your set-up. Boxes within boxes, toys and treats beneath towels, a child's play box filled with plastic balls surrounding the treats or toy. Spread the items over a wider area, create obstacles to make access to the activities more challenging, and so on.

I CAN RESIST!

In this game your dog learns to resist the presented temptation and look to you for a different, reliable reward instead. This lesson is fantastic for building impulse control skills. Those dogs that can be successfully asked to 'leave' items they should not touch have the joy of being granted more freedom in numerous situations.

WHAT YOU'LL NEED

- A selection of treats of various value to your dog
- A variety of toys
- Some items that your dog really covets but should never touch – perhaps your glove, shoe, remote control etc.

Get ready

Begin this game by preparing a selection of small treats. Ideally, have your treat pouch to hand so that you can access rewards quickly when needed.

Choose an area free from other distractions, and if you have other dogs, separate them for now.

Decide on the verbal cue you will use later on in this game. 'Leave' is commonly chosen, but if you have been using this word for a while without really enforcing it, it is best to start afresh with a new word.

Get steady

Find a comfortable position in front of your dog. You will need to be calm and patient during this game and want to avoid fidgeting or moving. Take a selection of the treats in one hand and close your fist around them.

Let's play!

Ask your dog to sit or lie down to begin. Hold the hand with the food at your dog's nose level or just below so that they can sniff it and understand that there are goodies inside.

Keep your hand steady, even if they nudge, paw at or sniff at your hand. Don't say anything and resist pulling away.

The moment your dog sits back or turns their head away, even if just a short distance, you should be ready and mark the movement with praise and then take a treat from your treat pouch with your other hand and reward them. By ignoring the temptation, other rewards will be on offer.

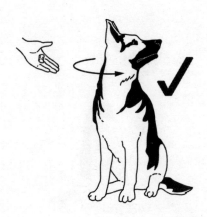

Repeat until your dog starts to move their head away more quickly from the fist holding the treats. Reward this choice each time. You should find that your dog also starts to turn or back away from the hand. Always praise and reward them from your other hand.

You can now start to say your cue word, 'leave', as your dog looks away from your hand. Continue to praise and reward every time they back off appropriately.

Progress to saying 'leave' when your dog glances at the hand holding the treats. If they have made the association with turning away and this verbal cue, you should find they disengage from the temptation to earn their reward that way.

Now begin to open the fist slowly to increase the lure of the treats held within. Most dogs are drawn to this, but, as they get closer, close your hand again to prevent access. Wait patiently and try not to move your hand, as this will draw their interest. As soon as your dog turns away you can praise them and offer a treat from the other hand.

Continue until you can open up your hand holding the treats in sight of your dog without them moving towards it. Praise and reward from your other hand. Your dog learns that by leaving the temptation they reliably get some goodies, but if they try to grab it, the treat disappears.

Now start to hold out your hand containing the treats at arm's length to the side of you, again waiting for your dog to turn away or look at you instead of trying to go to the food. Once your dog can do this, make it more interesting by moving your hand downwards towards the floor. Many dogs will assume something going onto the floor is worth exploring. If your dog gets up, close

your hand around the treat and gently ask them to come back into their sit/down position to restart.

Continue to practise until your dog is able to resist, even if you place the treat on the floor.

Now, while your dog is distracted in another direction, progress to placing some treats on the floor near to you.

As they approach and notice the treats, use your 'leave' cue and be ready to cover them with your hand or foot if they attempt to move to take them. Again, any movement away from the treats will earn praise and rewards from your pouch.

Eventually, your dog should be able to resist moving towards dropped food, discarded shoes and any other object they should not pick up.

TOP TRAINING TIPS

🐾 Increase your dog's desire for the item they have to leave by using tastier foods in your hand.

🐾 The same concept and routine applies to toys, but unless they are very small, these can easily be taken hold of and a tug game attempted. Therefore, wait until your dog has understood the basic concept with treats first. Reward from your pouch as usual. If you find that your dog prefers toys in this set-up, you can present a second toy instead and throw it for your dog to catch or chase as a reward instead.

🐾 Begin with less exciting toys to resist and build up to those they love. Bounce the toy in your hand to really create temptation.

🐾 Bring on the challenge! In real life you might not be standing directly beside the thing you wish your dog to ignore. Therefore, begin to step away from the item to create more distance before praising your dog and rewarding them for directing their focus to you. In the scenario above it can be useful to throw the treat or toy you are using as a reward in a direction away from the original temptation, so that you can distract your dog while you safely retrieve the item. Doing so reduces the risk that your dog will take the opportunity to gobble the treat or grab the toy on the way past. As your dog's skill grows you can create challenges, such as having to walk past the tempting item, but this should not be attempted until they are masters of resistance in the easier stages.

FOOD FORAGE FUN

Our busy routines often mean that we organize our dog's mealtimes to occur at set times, from a convenient bowl. This is not a natural situation and skips their need to seek out their food. Similarly, the convenience of processed dog food makes consuming it faster and uses fewer natural actions too. You are probably aware of more toys being on the market now that engage your dog while they eat. Perhaps you are not sure if they work, suit your dog, or what reasoning lies behind such items. Ultimately, benefits come from the option of using natural instincts to seek, obtain and consume food, using time and energy that would otherwise be left unused, leaving your dog potentially unfulfilled.

WHAT YOU'LL NEED
- A range of treats and safe food items
- A range of purpose-bought or DIY activity toys to suit your dog's size and behaviour

Get ready

Start out fairly easy. If you make this the most challenging way ever invented to access food, it is likely that your dog will give up before they gain any benefit, just as we would if our first attempt at a new sport or hobby was judged against world champion standards. If your dog has only ever been fed from a bowl, they will need to learn how to access food in other ways, starting with smaller portions at first. Some breeds and individuals are going to be naturally more instinctive at this than others, but most dogs can learn if given incentive and if the game is built up to be associated with fun.

Do you prefer to invest in a range of purpose-made toys? There are many different options for all styles of play: rubber toys in which you stuff food for your dog to chew and lick out; plastic toys to hold dry kibble or treats in and that require your dog to roll and move about so as to dispense them; snuffle mats that encourage sniffing and foraging for treats among folds and strands of material knotted into a mat; or textured bowls and silicon mats with a range of surfaces, which your dog has to lick to access the food you have smeared on to these. In all choices, you can start with easy ones and increase the challenge, perhaps having to consider a range of food choices each time.

Do you like DIY activities? There are many ways to create your own planned (or spontaneous) activities for your dog. These have the benefit of being cheap and using spare cardboard boxes, cardboard inner tubes, paper packing material, old towels or any other dog-safe objects you might have in your home to create food dispensing and foraging opportunities.

Get steady

Choose your toy. Make sure it is the right size for your dog to avoid accidental ingestion or choking. Dog toys often come in soft rubber options or harder versions for tougher chewers. If you know your dog is a hard chewer, opt for larger versions of the tough toys.

Choose the food filler. What really gets your dog excited? Will this game be a way to feed them their

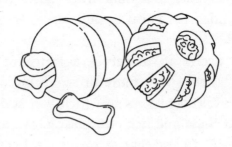

regular meal or is it an opportunity to engage them while they have some extras? Start with small amounts of any new food to avoid stomach upsets. There are often ways to bring in your dog's usual food, even if it's a dry biscuit version. Soaking, crushing and mixing with other ingredients can make even basic dog food very versatile.

Prior preparation

It might be easier to prepare a range of toys at the same time, particularly if you are filling them with soft meat, yoghurt, bananas, purée or other fresh fillings. You can then freeze these or refrigerate until they are needed.

If you have an empty plastic bottle you can create your own treat dispenser. Remove and discard the lid, as this is a choking hazard, then fill with some treats and present it to your dog. As they move it about, the treats will start to fall out. If your dog finds this option difficult to dispense many treats then you can carefully cut additional holes along the side – large enough that your treats can fall out one by one, but not so large that all the contents will be dispensed within the first roll. (Be careful that your cut holes have no sharp ragged edges and consider filing down any areas that might be problematic.) Now you have a DIY treat dispenser option for wherever you are. Your dog can play with this and enjoy the food and the sounds the bottle makes too. Refill if it is in good condition, otherwise dispose of it and start with a new one next time.

Faster options

Treat towel
Idea 1

Take your towel and spread it out on a table. Scatter some treats over the surface, then roll it up along the longest side. Once you have it rolled into a long tube, tie it into a knot and then present to your dog to unravel.

Idea 2

Take an old towel or sheet and lay it flat on the floor. Scatter some dry treats over the surface. Hold the centre of the material in one hand and twist so that it starts to come together in a whirl. Keep twisting in one direction until the entire towel is pulled together into a spiral shape, covering the treats in its folds. Now your

dog will have to nose, and dig into the material to access the hidden treats.

Cardboard tube instant treat dispenser

Grab an empty cardboard tube. Crush and fold in one end, then drop some treats into the other. Now crush that end too and, voilà, you have a simple treat dispenser. Your dog will chew and shred the card to access the goodies inside, so consider whether your dog is likely to consume the card before you start this game. Some dogs are more prone to consuming non-food items than others; this should shape the choices you make.

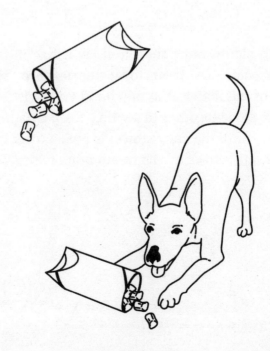

Egg box challenge

Scatter some treats inside an empty egg carton and close it. Begin with one carton, then build up to setting out several at once. Again, always consider your dog's propensity for consuming materials they shred.

Mystery box

Utilize the spare boxes left over from deliveries. All shapes and sizes can be useful. Ideally, choose those that are not dyed, and remove staples, tape and all glue strips before letting your dog have access. Small packages can be folded up around some treats. Larger boxes can be filled with some paper packing (again choose non-dyed paper to avoid risks of toxicity if any is consumed) or plastic balls if you have them. Scatter treats inside the box and you will now have a foraging game for your dog to enjoy.

Let's play!

Present your choice of activity and initially remain nearby to verbally encourage your dog to explore. You might time these activities for periods where you want your dog to be occupied, when you are busy and cannot play with them directly, and to encourage more independent play, which is important for some dogs that are naturally inclined to seek interaction constantly.

TOP TRAINING TIPS

🐾 Create some yummy popsicles for hot days by freezing a variety of your dog's favourite foods in ice-cube trays (choose a cube size appropriate for your dog). Toss these onto the lawn, or lay them on an old towel for your dog to work on without creating too much mess.

🐾 Let your dog figure out these games for themselves rather than you helping them to get the treats, or they may always rely on you to do this. Verbal encouragement and praise can help to get them started in developing their skills.

🐾 Bring on the challenge! If your dog is a great explorer and loves to dive in and get the treats, you can increase the challenge by filling smaller boxes and putting these inside larger ones so that there are several layers to work through. This might create some mess but your dog will be occupied for a good length of time and should be fairly satisfied afterwards!

🐾 Another challenge would be to roll the cardboard tube or egg cartons inside the towel for an extra layer of difficulty.

HOME AGILITY

Most dogs can enjoy agility, even if it's just some simple components. While plenty of dog-and-owner pairs compete and spend a lot of time engaging in this sport, dogs of all shapes and sizes, and owners with less time, can have fun playing this at home in their garden or even indoors.

Sometimes playing games outside is not possible due to the weather or your own health. Depending on the size of your dog and your home, this game may not be suitable, so if your dog is large and space tight, opt for a more calm, focused game instead.

WHAT YOU'LL NEED

- Treats to use as a reward for your dog
- Items to go over, under, around or through – you could use agility equipment or your own furniture
- Non-slip flooring or mats

Get ready

It helps if your dog has a knowledge of basic obedience commands before you teach agility, as this allows you to engage with them more effectively.

Clear a safe and spacious area where you can set up your agility course. If playing inside, make sure the area is free from fragile or valuable items that could be knocked over or damaged during the game. In your garden, ensure that your dog is away from greenhouses, fragile pots and garden canes.

You don't need to purchase official agility equipment to enjoy this game, as you can create the challenge with a range of items.

Tunnel

You might have a child's play-tunnel, but a large cardboard box with both ends open, or a tunnel created by using blankets or sheets draped over furniture, will work too.

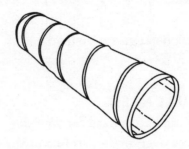

Jumps

You can create a jump with a plastic cone and pole, or make one with broomsticks and low-lying sturdy objects. It is important never to set jumps too high for your dog, and to pay particular attention when your dog is new and unfamiliar with jumping.

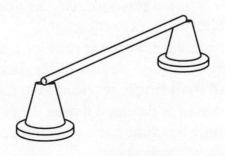

Weave poles

Create a line-up of upright objects such as cones, buckets, or even old water bottles refilled with water or sand to create weave poles. On grass you can use garden canes (consider safety ends to prevent any injury to you or your dog) or actual weave poles. Space them apart to allow your dog to navigate through them.

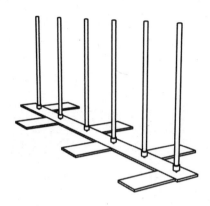

Balance beam

Place a long, sturdy, narrow object like a low wooden board on the ground for your dog to walk along.

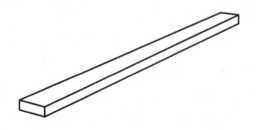

Station

Set up a designated mat as a starting point and as places for your dog to pause or perform specific behaviours as they work around your course. Small dogs can use a plastic footstool as their station and larger dogs might use a garden seat. Decide, depending on your dog and the facilities available, and always consider the safety risks.

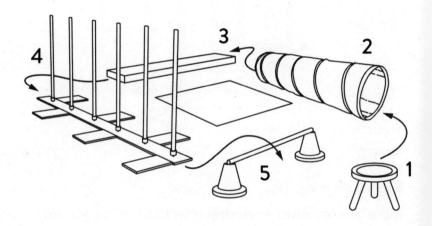

Get steady

Consider the space you are playing in and shape the route around the most sensible use of this area. Your dog will need space to move between activities, jump and land, so try not to jam in too many close together.

Each activity should be introduced as an individual activity and ensure that your dog is safe and comfortable before adding in more steps. Starting with something simple like a low jump or a tunnel will help you to get your dog into the swing of things and build confidence. You can then link these activities together in a designated order to create a more complex course.

With each step use treats, toys or enthusiastic praise to encourage your dog to explore and interact with the equipment. Focus on getting your timing right so that you are rewarding the precise action you want each time.

Let's play!

Use your positive reinforcement approach to shape your dog's behaviour around each component of the course. You decide on the order of the course and your dog will rely on your signals to know which one comes next. Make sure that you have taught a final activity where your dog gets rewarded; you can build the course around this. This means you choose which activity will be the end-point – perhaps dropping down on a mat or passing a finishing post – and then practise this and offer the reward after completion. Build the remainder of the course and always reward your dog when they reach the end.

There are two ways to teach a course or routine: from starting action 1, then 2, then 3 to the final action, or starting with the final point, then the second-last action, then the preceding one all the way back to the starting point. This might seem unusual, but such a backwards approach (or 'back-chaining') can be very effective because the dog gets familiar with the end-point of the game first; the trigger for the reward is consistent, it has been practised often, and they know that when they get to that specific stage the reward will be given. This is nicely predictable, whereas with normal forward-chaining (where you start from the beginning and work towards the end), some dogs become frustrated as more and more activities get in the way of the arrival of the final reward. Having the goalpost change so often can cause problems with maintaining motivation.

Once you have strung two actions together, the reward should come after both parts have been completed. This will prevent your dog from deviating in between to receive their reward. Encourage calm focus by building in pauses on your targeting mats or platforms in between other activities.

Be mindful of the duration of your sessions. Keep them short and fun to maintain your dog's interest and prevent them from becoming fatigued and injured. Frequent but brief sessions will yield better results and make the game more enjoyable for your dog in the long run. Remember the impact too much high-arousal activity (page 25) can have on your dog's stress levels.

TOP TRAINING TIPS

🐾 Vary the layout and difficulty level as your dog becomes more comfortable and able. Rearrange the equipment, add new challenges, and incorporate different commands to keep your dog engaged and mentally stimulated.

🐾 Bring on the challenge! As you work on each activity you can adjust it to suit your dog's capabilities; for example, by raising a bar or adding in a more complex manoeuvre. As you do this they will become more reliant on your careful signalling to guide them to the correct activity and to ensure they take the necessary pauses. If your dog loves this, there is likely to be a local trainer who can offer to work you through more formal training, either as part of a group or one to one.

GO AROUND

This game teaches your dog to go out around various obstacles. This can be brought into your walks to increase interest and exercise opportunities. If you want to engage in activities such as agility or other formal training, you will find this is something you use often. It can be a slow action or super-fast, depending on your dog, but should be fun either way.

WHAT YOU'LL NEED
- A selection of training treats
- An object for your dog to move around (a cone, box, stool etc.)

Get ready

Ensure that your dog is comfortable around the object you are working with. If they are wary at all, give them time and praise and reward any interaction they have with it. If the concern remains, consider choosing something else to begin with and once your dog is confident with the game you can come back and try again.

Get steady

Stand beside the item and encourage your dog to come close to you.

Let's play!

Holding a treat in one hand, lure your dog to walk around the object in your chosen direction. As they follow the treat around, praise them and release the treat.

Repeat a few times until the movement around the object becomes faster and easier for your dog. Always remember to praise and reward them for being successful.

Add in your chosen verbal cue (e.g. 'around') as they start to move around the object. Praise and reward for doing the right response. Repeat so they get used to connecting the cue with the action.

Now you want to fade out your lure so that your dog does not become too reliant on it. Start by giving the hand gesture but without holding any treats. Offer the reward from your pouch when your dog gets it right.

Increasing the distance between you and the object is the next stage in this game. Begin a step away from it and gesture while giving your 'around' cue. Praise and reward well for correct responses. Build up the distance gradually, being mindful of any other distractions occurring and choosing the difficulty based on what you know your dog can manage.

TOP TRAINING TIPS

🐾 If you notice any confusion as you start to fade the lure or work from distances, go back a stage and practise before increasing the difficulty more slowly.

🐾 Bring on the challenge! Now your dog can move around an object from various distances you can start to apply the concept to new obstacles within and outside the home. You can send them out to go around trees, posts or benches while on a walk as a way to keep them engaged and active.

BALL SKILLS

This activity can be an entertaining game for the garden, but can also be developed into a competitive activity called Treibball. This canine sport is becoming increasingly popular and involves herding large exercise balls into a goal using the dog's body and nose. Whether you do this just for fun at home, or wish to compete, dogs of all shapes and sizes can participate.

WHAT YOU'LL NEED
- A selection of treats for rewarding your dog
- A large yoga ball or other large plastic ball
- Plastic cones, or other objects to create goalposts

Get ready

This game is much easier if your dog already has an understanding of a couple of other activities. The first one is targeting with their nose – if they have not done any of this please look at the targeting tasks section for some initial guidance (see page 75). Another very helpful activity to teach first is the 'go around' game (see page 106).

Ensure that your dog is comfortable with the exercise balls and let them sniff and investigate them.

Get steady

Stand or sit with the exercise ball held securely between your legs. Initially you will be working on encouraging your dog to make firm contact with the ball and it's important that it doesn't move yet.

Let's play!

Encourage your dog to push on the ball with their nose – use a target marker or tape to encourage contact if this helps to get you started. Ideally your dog should always be pushing towards you, so position your target, if using one, thoughtfully.

Try to focus on your timing, since you want to reward pushing with the nose and not any open-mouthed contact or pawing. You might need to pay attention and shape your dog to push in the centre to begin with. Getting the foundation skills right will be advantageous going forwards.

Now you will need to stabilize your ball so that you have freedom to move. The easiest way to do this is by rolling up a towel into a sausage shape and then creating a circle for the ball to sit inside.

Stand close to the ball at first and encourage your dog to push; they will have to put some effort in to push it over the towel barrier. Practise until your dog can easily go to the ball and push it towards you.

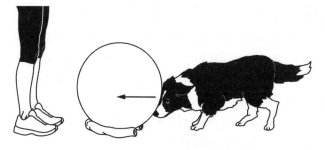

Stand a step back from the ball and repeat. Gradually increase your distance from the ball so that your dog learns that moving it towards you is part of the game.

Some dogs will benefit from having a narrow area to push the ball down at first as this helps to minimize movement to the sides. Hallways or between furniture can be helpful for this. Try to move on to new locations as soon as your dog appears to understand how to move the ball.

For the next stage you should come closer to the ball again and call your dog to stand beside you. Send them out to go 'around' the ball. As they move behind the ball, give your cue to push it.

Building confidence that they can move the ball, even when it gets stuck in a corner or by an obstacle, is an important part of the game. You can help your dog to overcome this challenge by practising with the ball sitting close to, but not directly against, an obstacle. Send your dog 'around' the ball to show them that they can still move there and encourage them to push it towards you if they can. As your dog learns this manoeuvring skill you can slowly move the starting position of the ball closer to the obstacle so that it becomes increasingly difficult to access the back of the ball. They will need to learn to shove and push with their shoulders in such a way that they can eventually get access and start moving the ball in the right direction.

When you move to practise in different locations remember to simplify the game to make it easier to succeed, gradually building up the necessary skills on the new terrain.

Add in hand and arm signals to help to guide your dog. If they need to move to one side of the ball or other, reaching out with your arm towards that side can help to provide information to guide them. Go back to basics when introducing these movements. Place the ball back into the towel circle so it doesn't roll away and position yourself on the opposite side to your dog. Using your right hand, gesture out towards that side of the ball to encourage your dog to move that way before giving your push cue. Hold off with the praise/click and treats until they have moved slightly around to the appropriate side and have pushed. Work on both sides until your dog understands that your gestures are guiding them.

Introducing the 'goal' will be the next stage in this

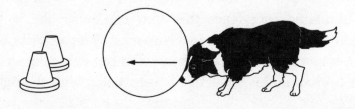

game. Set these up and position yourself between the goal markers. Position the ball directly in front of the goal and encourage your dog to push it the short distance between the posts. Remember, since you have changed the criteria, you should set up the game to ensure that success comes easily for your dog.

Now add distance by positioning the ball gradually further from the goal. Your dog will have to push further to get through the goal markers. Give your directional signalling to help them to move it towards you.

TOP TRAINING TIPS

🐾 Some dogs struggle with the concept of going around and pushing from the other side of the ball. If this happens then you should work separately on encouraging, or targeting, your dog to move to and stop on a mat. Then position this mat behind the ball and send them out to stand on it. Once this routine is understood, progress to the push action from there. Chaining different actions together like this is a common component of more complex training and while it involves additional steps, overall it provides clear instructions for your dog to follow and can avoid problems with confusion or frustration.

🐾 Bring on the challenge! Mastered the game with one ball? Now it is time to add in more. The game of Treibball actually uses eight balls – your neighbour won't believe their eyes when they look out into your garden and see this game in action.

CLEAN UP!

Throughout this book you are encouraged to play and provide opportunities for your dog to engage with toys. With this fun comes a little chaos and the potential for toys everywhere, so why not train your dog to help tidy up afterwards? The result is a happy dog from all the games and a happy owner from having order restored at the end of the session. Of course, there are a few different options for this game: you could, for example, teach your dog to take items of rubbish to the bin for you. The game should depend on your dog's habits; if they are, or have been, a bin-raider, you might want to avoid teaching them to engage with rubbish further. But whether it's their toys or your empty plastic drinks bottle, you can have fun teaching them to take it to the box or bin and do their bit to keep your living space tidy.

WHAT YOU'LL NEED
- A toy (something easy to pick up) or an empty plastic bottle
- A toy-box/toy-basket or a bin
- Treats

Get ready

Focus on the individual components of the game so that you can be confident that your dog knows what is being asked of them during this activity. There are some prerequisites that would be useful to work on before trying this game. These include 'take it' and 'drop' (see

page 72). If you have enjoyed the targeting games, you may focus instead on targeting your dog to approach and pick up toys or items from the floor without any new verbal cues. Choose the approach that suits you and your dog's preferred training style most.

Select a toy-box, or a suitable bin where you will teach your dog to drop the item. It is helpful if the box/bin is low enough for them to drop the item in easily, or the early stages of the training may be more challenging than necessary.

The toy or item you work with should be easy for your dog to pick up and not something that triggers overexcitement and a play session of its own.

Get steady

These instructions will focus on putting toys away, but the same steps can be used if you are teaching your dog to clear up rubbish. Be patient and work through each stage carefully so that your dog fully understands.

Let's play!

Sit on the floor and practise asking your dog to pick up the toy from the floor and bring it to you. When they are directly in front of you, give your marker signal (a 'yes' or a click) – it is likely that this will cause your dog to drop the toy in order to take the treat from you. Some dogs need you to say 'drop' at this stage. Don't worry if this is your dog's habit, as this cue can be phased out later. Repeat a few times so that your dog is used to picking up the toy and approaching you before dropping it in front of you for their reward.

Position the toy-box directly in front of you, ideally where your dog has been dropping the toy in previous practice sessions. Place the toy on the floor on your dog's side of the box. Then get your dog's attention and direct them to the toy, which they should pick up since you have practised this previously. Hold your hand over the box to encourage them to approach you. In an ideal scenario your dog will approach and hold the toy over the box, at which point give your 'yes' or click, which will cause your dog to release the toy and it should fall into the box.

If this does not happen immediately, don't worry. Some dogs will drop the toy close to the edge of the box at first. This can be rewarded and then shaped towards the desired behaviour; consider where you were holding your hand, the direction your dog was approaching from and so on to determine if there are small changes that might influence their behaviour. Some dogs respond well to being rewarded directly over the box at first so that the release of the toy is encouraged in exactly the right place.

Repeat by replacing the same toy on the floor each time. As you progress and the drop into the box is occurring more reliably, you may find that tossing the treat away from you helps your dog to 'reset' their position ready to approach again.

Now begin to delay your reward signal until the toy falls into the box. Repeat until your dog is confidently picking up the toy and placing it into the receptacle. Once this is happening you can start to position it further away from the box to build up the need to pick up and approach the box from different angles. Progress slowly so that your dog is set up for success.

Begin to change your position, sitting on different sides of the box, standing beside it, a step away from it and so on. Your dog will learn that the rules of the game apply no matter where you are positioned.

Now you can begin to work on building this skill using other toys. Start with one new toy and gradually build up to include others. Go back to some easier steps at first so that your dog finds it easy to apply the previously learned lesson to this new item. Small, easy steps set your dog up for success and a confident response. After they have learned the game with a range of toys, they should be able to generalize to others in the same situation.

Your dog is now ready to hear your verbal cue. As they move to pick up the toy, say your chosen cue (e.g. 'clean up') and follow the routine as above. If you have been routinely giving other cues to get your dog to 'take it', then begin by saying 'clean up, take it', and over time your dog should start to respond as you say 'clean up' alone, as this will be paired with the 'take it' response.

TOP TRAINING TIPS

🐾 If your dog loses focus on the toy or item you are working on, pick it up between each practice session and place it back down. This naturally draws their attention to it again in the early stages.

🐾 Wherever you can, fade out initial verbal signals such as 'take it' as early as possible. Once your dog has understood the game, try to do this.

🐾 Bring on the challenge! Some super-smart dogs can be taught to target a pedal bin lever with their feet to open the bin, then place an item inside. This will require breaking down the process into separate parts and then combining the two (see page 75 for targeting skills). Avoid this if your dog might forage in bins containing dangerous items.

GET YOUR LEAD

Teaching your dog to help with their daily routine by bringing you their lead can be a fun addition to your interactions. Going out on walks is such a fun activity that most dogs are more than happy to engage in this game.

WHAT YOU'LL NEED
- Your dog's lead
- A selection of treats

Get ready

While training for this game, the lead will need to be placed where your dog can access it, preferably in a designated spot near the door or in a specific area where you want them to retrieve it from. This game will be easier if you have already trained the concept of 'take it' (page 72).

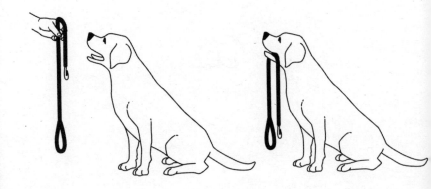

Get steady

Practise your 'take it' cue with the lead so that your dog is used to taking hold of it in their mouth. Begin by holding it and gradually move it onto the floor, or a surface your dog can easily reach. Reward them each time they take the lead into their mouth. Build up until they can hold it. Usually the dog will release the item when they receive the reward from you, but some dogs might have to follow a specific 'drop it' routine (page 72) to avoid a tug-of-war situation.

Let's play!

Place the lead down and encourage your dog to pick it up and drop it in your hand. Gradually increase the distance between you and the lead so that your dog has to pick up the lead and step towards you with it. Depending on the size of your dog they may feel very comfortable picking it up, others might be worried about it dragging under their feet. In the short term it may help to fold and tie up the lead to make it easy to lift and carry.

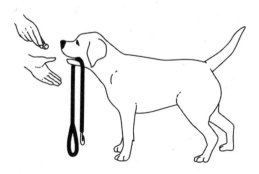

Continue to develop this game whereby your dog has to go to and pick up the lead in various positions, and then must approach you with it to earn their rewards. It can be useful to ask another family member to help by gently restraining your dog while they see you position the lead and move away. This builds up a little excitement and often creates more enthusiasm, which you can reinforce well.

You can begin to present your verbal cue, 'get your lead', as your dog approaches the lead. Repeat and reward as usual when your dog is successful. Start to give the cue slightly earlier until you can give it and your dog turns to look for the lead.

Once you are ready, play this game before clipping the lead onto your dog's collar and stepping out on a walk. For many dogs this is the ultimate reward and will keep them

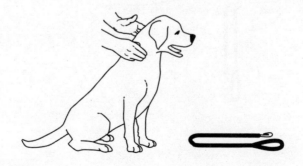

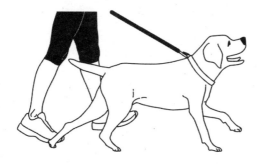

playing again. If your dog is wary of going on walks then you can associate this with being taken to a place where they are comfortable, like the garden or out in the car.

TOP TRAINING TIPS

🐾 If your dog picks up and brings you their lead in between training sessions, you should praise and reward them for doing so. In the later stages the reward will only come when you have given your 'get the lead' cue, but initially they should be encouraged for all interaction. If you don't want this, then place the lead out of sight and reach.

🐾 If your dog normally wears a harness, this can be fitted in advance, and when the lead is brought to you, clip it on and go out as usual. Consider teaching your dog to fetch their harness too.

🐾 Bring on the challenge! Now you can combine this lesson with teaching your dog to open the cupboard or drawer where it is kept.

CHAPTER 3

LET'S BE SOCIABLE

The games in this section are not solely intended to make your dog engage with people. Being sociable involves being relaxed, helpful and entertaining. The benefits from any game will depend on your dog and their starting point. Engaging in reward-based training of any sort can improve confidence and support your relationship, therefore naturally improving sociability skills. Be mindful that 'sociable' responses for one dog will involve direct contact and engagement, while for another their social limits may be more about relaxing around people at a distance. Work with your individual dog and see where your adventures together can lead to.

WAVE HELLO AND GOODBYE

This is a simple trick for most healthy dogs and a fun way to have them follow a known cue around friends and family. This routine might build in positive emotions when people arrive or leave the home, and change the need for some people to want to touch and fuss over the dog to say goodbye.

WHAT YOU'LL NEED
- Some tasty treats to reward your dog
- Some dogs will prefer to work on a mat or carpeted area

Get ready

To learn to 'wave', your dog will first need to know how to move into the sitting position on cue. Most dogs learn to do this early on, though many don't do so reliably when their owners request it. See page 66 for guidance on this.

Decide what sort of 'wave' you want to teach: a one-pawed hello, a two-pawed wave or an enthusiastic standing wave? Your dog's physical shape and fitness will determine what they are most suited for and you can always work through all the options if you wish.

Get steady

Position yourself so that your dog is sitting comfortably in front of you. Make sure you have easy access to your treats.

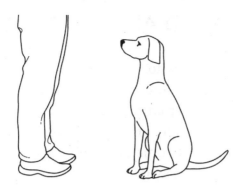

Let's play!
One-paw hello

This one is easy if your dog already knows how to give a paw. If not, most dogs can be quickly taught to do so. Hold your treats out in one hand at your dog's chest level but do not release. Your dog is likely to sniff, nudge and eventually paw at your hand to try to access the food. The moment that the paw lifts up, praise your dog and release the food.

Now repeat, making sure that you only praise and treat when the paw is off the floor.

Over several trials, gradually hold your hand further from your dog's body so that they have to reach up higher towards your hand in order to get the praise and reward. See 'Two-paw wave', below, for the rest of the exercise.

Two-paw wave

Encourage your dog into a sitting position and then take a treat in one hand and, starting at your dog's nose, slowly move it upwards and backwards so that your dog has to lean back and lift their front paws off the ground slightly. As soon as you see them do this, praise and reward them with the treat. Repeat until your dog is more comfortable sitting up with their front paws off the ground when you lure them in this way.

Once your dog is moving into your chosen position (one- or two-paw) fairly quickly, you should begin to introduce your verbal cue for the action. This could be 'wave', 'big wave', 'say hi' or similar. Start with your lure and as your dog begins to move, say your chosen word. This will begin the pairing process between action and cue.

Fade out your lure by repeating the usual hand movements but without holding the treat. Then slowly make the hand movements less and less exaggerated over subsequent practice attempts. Remember to always reward your dog with a treat and praise for correctly responding.

TOP TRAINING TIPS

🐾 Be mindful of how many repetitions you do, as sitting up repeatedly can be tiring.

🐾 Bring on the challenge! You can develop a more deliberate waving action by moving your hand away slightly as your dog reaches out to paw at it. As they reach again, or start the 'wave' motion, you can then praise and reinforce. From now on, reward after two 'wave' motions and consider building up further if desired.

🐾 Feeling enthusiastic? Lure your dog to sit up higher by holding the treat above their head so that they have to sit back on their hind legs and stretch to reach it. Gradually shape this response and build your dog's ability to hold this position. Be mindful of any physical difficulties that could be exacerbated in this position. Some canine body shapes, including some with deeper chests or longer backs, are not especially well suited to this version.

CAN I GO OUT?

It can be useful to teach your dog to signal when they would like to go out into your garden for a toilet break. While some dogs make it very obvious that this is what they wish to do, others have more subtle signals, which can be easily missed if you are otherwise occupied. Having a bell to catch your attention can help improve communication for some dogs.

WHAT YOU'LL NEED
- A large training bell, electronic bell button or a set of metal bells to hang from the door handle, or next to the doorway
- A supply of treat rewards

Get ready

First, you will need to be sure that your dog is comfortable being around the bells and the sound they make. If they approach to sniff this new object, praise and reward them. All interaction is encouraged at this stage.

Get steady

Position your bell by the door where you wish them to exit. Make sure it is securely fastened and will not come off when your dog interacts with it. Electronic buttons should not be able to slip along the floor.

Let's play!

If your dog is not doing so already, lure them close to the bell with a treat so that they make contact and trigger the sound. Immediately praise and give the treat. Repeat this stage over several short sessions until your dog is confidently nudging the bells to earn a treat.

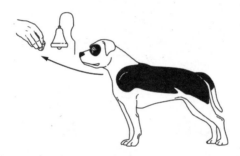

Now you are ready to teach your dog to ring the bell to go outside. This occurs via pairing the bell-ringing with the door-opening. Begin when you know your dog

is wanting to go outside, such as by timing it alongside their regular bathroom breaks. Before you open the door to let them go outside, encourage them to ring the bell. As soon as they do, offer praise and then open the door to let them go out.

Be prepared that you will need to prompt your dog each time for a while until they learn that ringing the bell leads to you opening the door. Get the whole family involved so that every break outside gets connected with ringing the bell.

TOP TRAINING TIPS

🐾 Gradually phase out the offer of treats so that eventually the reward your dog anticipates is being let outside. You can praise them as you respond to the signal.

🐾 Bring on the challenge! Once your dog knows that the bell-ringing will reliably signal to you to let them out, you will need to be careful that it does not become a means to elicit attention at all times of day or night. If there are times you do not want to let your dog outside, remove the bells so that your dog cannot use them (and fail to get a response). Eventually, the bell-ringing should be associated with the toileting-need and your dog shouldn't feel the need to ring incessantly!

CHOOSING A GAME

Over recent years there has been growing interest in teaching dogs to communicate via talking buttons. Dogs such as Stella and Bunny have become famous on social media by using apparently complex language to convey desires and thoughts. While science is still seeking the answers for how much dogs really understand when they use word buttons to communicate with their owners, it is true that they can learn to connect specific cues with activities. Therefore, for this game you can teach your dog to request specific games by choosing the connected signal. Having a means to specifically request a particular game can alleviate potential stress and frustration.

WHAT YOU'LL NEED
- A set of recordable training buttons (available in various numbers from many sellers – the type and size of the ideal button will vary depending on your dog)
- A specific toy or activity that you wish your dog to request via the button

Get ready

First, you will want to introduce the button to your dog. You want them to feel familiar with it and comfortable enough to sniff and investigate.

Use your targeting techniques (see page 75) to guide your dog towards pressing the button with their nose or paw. While some dogs will be encouraged to do this with the lure of treats, this is something that you will

want to move away from very quickly in this game, otherwise your dog may always press the button for a treat and not progress to understanding the action it signifies in full.

Get steady

Although you might feel very keen, initially start with only one button. Assign a specific game to this particular button. Once you link this button and the action you should not switch the meaning, or your dog is likely to feel confused. There is usually a recording setting to allow you to clearly state the game name associated with this button. This will tell you what your dog is asking for later on.

The game or activity the button signals should be distinct and very clear for your dog to learn. For example, always signifying either a ball, Kong or tuggy game.

Keep the toy associated with the button close to hand while you are training for this game so that you can respond appropriately every time your dog presses the button. So, if the button signifies a ball game, you should have a ball (or several) nearby so that you can immediately agree and throw the ball for your dog.

Let's play!

Ideally, the button should be positioned close to an area where the associated activity can take place. So, next to the toy-box, or near to the door if the button indicates a desire to go outside.

If your dog picks up the ball without pressing the button first, you can model the behaviour by going and pressing the button that plays the recording of you saying 'ball game' and then playing the game. Gradually increase the criteria for reinforcement, requiring your dog to press the button more firmly and intentionally each time. Practise the training sessions regularly to reinforce the behaviour. Be patient and consistent with your training efforts and be prepared to respond every time your dog presses the button to request this game.

TOP TRAINING TIPS

🐾 Begin with very distinct concepts such as connecting the button with a specific game, or activity.

🐾 If the button is available and your dog presses it, you should be prepared to respond with the appropriate game.

🐾 Bring on the challenge! Once the association is established you can introduce additional buttons, with new meanings. Now your dog can start to communicate with you regarding what they want to do. Who knows how far this will go? Some claim their dogs can use buttons to explain their dreams!

CLOSE THE DOOR

This multi-step game is both fun and useful if you are feeling rather lazy yourself. Your dog will learn to go to a door and push it closed with their nose or paw on cue. After all this training, perhaps you will have earned the rest!

WHAT YOU'LL NEED
- Selection of tasty treats
- A sticky note, sticker or alternative target mark

Get ready

This game is easier if your dog already has some response to target training (see page 75). The ideal target for this game is something that can be stuck to the door, such as a sticky note or some brightly coloured tape. If this item is new to your dog, spend some time bringing their focus to it. Hold it in your hand and encourage them to approach and touch the target with either their nose or their paw (depending on the size of your dog, decide which option will allow them to close the door

most easily). Each time they come and touch the target, you should click or praise and offer a treat.

Get steady

Practise until your dog is efficiently pressing the target each time. Hold it in different positions so that they become confident and gradually move it so that your hand is close to the door.

Let's play!

Now attach your target to the door at a height that allows your dog to press on it easily (head height for nose contact and lower chest for paw presses). Every time they make contact with the target on the door you should mark, praise and reward.

To progress with the game your dog will have to start to push harder on the target marker. Open the door slightly and begin to reward them only when they touch the target sufficiently that the door is moved. Practise over several short sessions so that your dog remains enthusiastic.

Gradually open the door a little further and reward as it is pushed closed. Every time your dog moves the door closed you should praise them and offer the reward.

Now move in a little closer again and add in your verbal cue (e.g. 'close the door') as you send your dog to contact the target. Ideally, this should be said just as they start to press on the door to allow for the closest association and least confusion. Practise until your dog is reliably moving towards the door when you give the cue.

Practise from further away again so that your dog moves towards the door before pressing it closed.

Always remember to reward them for successful actions – though now you can wait until the door is pushed shut before you offer this.

Once your dog is confidently closing the door on your command, it's time to fade out the target. Begin by making the target smaller, then gradually fade it out completely over several sessions. This might mean cutting or folding the marker to make it smaller. If, at any time, your dog struggles without the target, go back a step and make the changes more gradual.

TOP TRAINING TIPS

🐾 Decide on the manner of contact with the door early. Is your dog likely to scratch the door and cause damage if they use their paw? If so, teach them to press with their nose or consider placing a more permanent protective layer at the contact area.

🐾 Bring on the challenge! Practise from various areas of the room as you would in a real-life situation where you wanted your dog to close the door. Other family members can join in the game, though remember to go back to easier stages for each new person. Reducing criteria is always important if your dog appears confused at any stage.

🐾 Generalize to other doors by practising in different rooms, using wardrobe doors and kitchen cupboards.

OPEN THE DOOR

Just as convenient as 'close the door', this game can be much more than just a fun trick. It can function as an important support option too.

WHAT YOU'LL NEED
- A tuggy-toy, or a knotted length of cloth/towel
- Treats to reward correct responses

Get ready

Safety considerations. Being able to open a door might be a nice game but it also has potential downsides. For most dogs this version of the game will involve internal doors and cupboards. You will need to ensure that any door your dog can open will only permit access to safe items and places. It is not advisable to teach them to pull open drawers that may fall out onto them, or to create steps to countertops or windows.

Decide on your verbal cue (e.g. 'open door', 'pull it'). It will help if your dog is already comfortable with grabbing and pulling on a tuggy or rope toy. Having a cue to start this game (e.g. 'tug-tug') can help to get your dog enthusiastic about the process.

The rope toy you use will need to be long enough that your dog can comfortably grab it, but also to allow sufficient space for the door to open without banging directly into your dog. If this occurs, your dog is likely to want to avoid playing this game, just as we would in those circumstances.

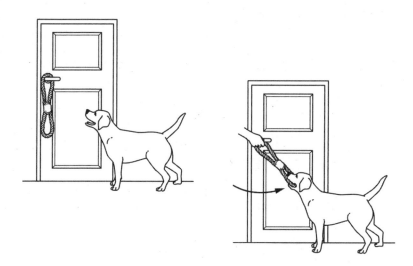

Get steady

Opening a door is much easier for a dog if they can pull on something other than the handle. By attaching the rope toy to the handle your dog will have a comfortable grip to work with while avoiding damage to the door.

Let's play!

You might have to hold or wiggle the attached tuggy to get your dog to grasp it at first. When they do, praise and encourage them to 'tug-tug'. Depending on the weight of the door, your dog may not have to pull very hard, so be nearby to prevent the door from swinging out too quickly at first. Gesture to the rope toy to encourage your dog to take hold of it. As they start to pull, say your chosen cue (e.g. 'open door'). As the door opens, praise and reward them.

Practise from various positions and distances from the door until your dog can confidently approach and pull on the rope when you signal to them to 'open door'.

TOP TRAINING TIPS

🐾 In between training sessions it is sensible to remove the rope-pull from the handle so that your dog does not open a door or cupboard when you are not expecting it. Once you have a particular cupboard or door that they are trained to open, and that you know is safe, you can leave the rope-pull attached.

🐾 Your dog might love you for it, but teaching them to open the food cupboard is probably not the best idea. While they are sure to be enthusiastic and keen to do extra practice, this could lead to excessive overindulgence.

🐾 Bring on the challenge! Once your dog has this game perfected you can move to additional doors, and consider combining it with other activities such as fetching their lead, bowl, your keys and so on.

BACK UP!

Being able to respond to directional cues can bring both practical and entertainment value. Your dog can back up if in a tight space, making space for people or other dogs. It can even increase your dog's awareness of their own movements.

WHAT YOU'LL NEED
• A selection of treats

Get ready

While you can teach this game anywhere, initially training within a narrow space such as a hallway or between furniture can actually speed up the early stages as it limits the potential mistakes your dog might make. The size of your dog will determine the appropriate space needed.

Get steady

Get your dog's attention so they are standing facing you. You can use treats as usual but can move to a toy if you prefer. Hold it slightly higher than their head height and

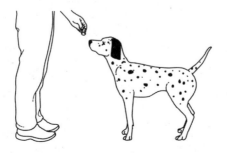

confidently step towards them. Normally the dog will then move backwards. As soon as they take one step back, say 'yes' or use your clicker to praise and give the treat. If your dog sits instead of stepping back, do not reward them. Instead, lure them back up again and try again, this time watching for the first tiny movement of a foot and then rewarding instantly. It may also help to hold the treat slightly lower down before stepping towards them since when the head is raised high, the bottom end naturally sinks down.

Let's play!

Practise this initial process several times until your dog starts to understand that moving backwards leads to a reward. Once they have picked up the idea and start to move backwards consistently for the treat, you can add a verbal cue, such as 'back up' or 'walk back'. Say this as you step towards your dog.

Repeat this simple routine over several sessions until your dog starts to associate the verbal cue with the action of stepping backwards.

Now you should start to fade out the treat lure so that

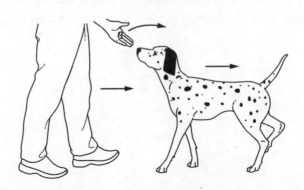

your dog does not remain reliant on it. Start as normal with your treat in your hand, then on the next repetition do the same movement without a treat in your hand but be prepared to reward them from your pouch as they start to back up.

For the next stage once more give your 'back up' cue as you step towards your dog. If they successfully move backwards, offer a treat. Next say your 'back up' cue while lifting your foot as if to step forwards but don't actually move – hopefully your dog will anticipate the routine and step back. You have now got the action without needing to move yourself. Practise so this becomes routine.

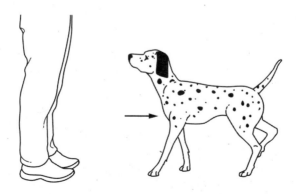

Increasing the number of steps or distance your dog backs up is your next aim. Delay your praise and reward until they have taken additional steps back, and encourage them with hand signals or cues if necessary until they get the idea. Go slowly, building the distance over many practice sessions.

With the backing-up action in place, you can now progress to a more open area. Be ready to reward small movements backwards again so that your dog continues to understand the task, despite the opportunity to make mistakes being significantly higher now.

TOP TRAINING TIPS

🐾 Once you have the basic lesson in place and your dog is consistently responding, try it in new locations with increased levels of distraction.

🐾 Bring on the challenge! Reversing can be helpful in a tight squeeze, if someone is unsure about your dog being close, or it can be built into a more complex training routine such as when doing home agility, or even if you feel inspired to create some heelwork to music routines.

WIPE YOUR PAWS

What could be better than an impressive trick that also has a real practical application? This one benefits all the dogs who need their paws dried off after a walk and is great for dogs who are already a bit sensitive about being handled there. While you work on reducing this worry, you can use this trick to get around the muddy prints on your floor.

WHAT YOU'LL NEED

- Some high-value treats that your dog loves to work for
- A large, absorbent towel or mat

Get ready

The first stage is to ensure your dog is relaxed and comfortable around the towel or mat you wish to use for this game. Many confident dogs will take this in their stride, but it is worth placing the towel or mat on the floor and encouraging your dog to approach and investigate. When they do, praise them and drop treats

for them to eat. This starts an association between the towel and enjoyable events.

Decide on your verbal cue for this game, e.g. 'wipe your paws'. You will need to be quick to capture the right wiping behaviours so decide in advance if you are going to use a clicker or a marker word to communicate with your dog.

Get steady

If your dog has already been taught to use their paws in previous targeting games then you already have the skills to get straight into this game. If this is new to your dog, you will have to encourage the initial scratch/ pawing response (see page 78).

If your dog is happy to use their paw to touch, there are different ways to encourage the scratching response. You could fold over part of the towel, hiding a treat underneath. As your dog explores and uses their front paws to uncover the treat, you can mark the behaviour, praise and reward them again. Other dogs will join in enthusiastically if you make some digging actions on

the towel with your hands; as soon as they join in, you can praise and reward them.

Back paws can be trickier to get moving. One way is to gently tickle the top of the foot so that your dog shuffles it; immediately mark this behaviour and reward them. This might take a bit of shaping to develop into a full wiping action.

Let's play!

Once you have your wiping action occurring fairly well, you should continue to develop this while adding in your verbal cue. Say 'wipe your paws' just as your dog starts to perform the actions, and then praise them. Remember to reward them for the wiping motion each time you practise.

Repeat this stage until your dog has connected the cue with the action. By now you probably have a fairly reliable paw swipe going on, but some dogs will be preferentially choosing one paw over the other. Try to delay the reward and encourage more enthusiastic wiping with multiple paws. If the back paws are mostly forgotten by your dog, teach this separately and join the two actions of front and back together later.

Gradually increase the duration of the wiping motion on the mat or towel before your praise and reward is presented.

Get into the habit of doing this activity every time you return from a walk. Keep the mat or towel handy in this place and build it into your routine so that your dog becomes used to it and is proficient when they are particularly wet or muddy.

TOP TRAINING TIPS

🐾 Bring on the challenge! Why not combine the paw wipe with a general body-drying activity? Teach your dog to lie down (page 69) and to roll over (page 202) on an absorbent mat, and their body will be easier to dry off after a rainy walk.

DOOR MANNERS

Teaching your dog to go and sit on their bed, or a mat, when the doorbell rings can be a useful behaviour for managing their excitement and reducing their impulse to rush to the door. This is a very exciting time and it is natural for them to want to rush there alongside you. Instead of getting frustrated and pulling them off guests, or holding them to prevent escape, this game can help you to instil a more manageable routine at the door while helping your dog to see it as another fun opportunity.

WHAT YOU'LL NEED
- A selection of treats for training
- A remote-controlled doorbell or a recording of the sound
- Someone to help out

Get ready

You should place your chosen dog bed or mat in a location they can easily access and where it will not block your movements as you go to the door. Consider safety – we never want our dog to be able to dash out of the door. For some dogs the best option is to position their bed behind a gate that you can close on your way to the door.

Can your dog go to their bed on cue? If not, this should be your first lesson. Use treats to lure your dog to their bed. As they step onto it say your cue (e.g. 'on your bed'), then praise and reward. Continue to practise the 'on your bed' cue until your dog is moving there quickly in order to earn the treat.

Then progress to fading out the lure. Gesture towards the bed as you were before but do not hold a treat in your hand. When your dog steps onto their bed immediately praise and offer a treat from your pouch. Gradually increase the distance between you and the bed, so your dog learns to go to their bed from different areas of the room.

Get steady

If your dog has not heard a doorbell before, this is ideal, as they will have no previously rehearsed response. Otherwise, you might wish to use a new tone or work through old habits in order to get the behaviour you are aiming for. If real-life visitors use the original ring and your training uses a new sound, eventually you will be able to swap over once the new habits are well established.

If the sound of the doorbell is connected with the 'on your bed' action, this game will go very smoothly. Be ready to encourage your dog to their bed. Play the doorbell, preferably at a lower volume than usual, and very enthusiastically encourage your dog to their bed with your 'on your bed' cue. As they step onto it, praise and reward profusely.

If your dog rushed off to the door instead of their bed, don't panic. No one is there, so you can wait for them to realize, then encourage them again to their bed for the reward.

Gradually increase the doorbell volume and continue to pair up your 'on your bed' cue with it. Eventually your dog will pair up these cues and the doorbell itself will begin to be the signal to go to the bed for rewards.

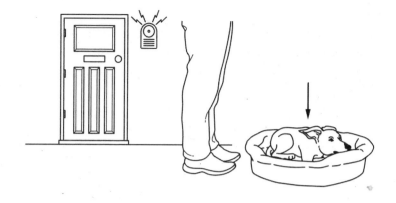

Modern doorbells often come with a wireless button allowing them to be rung while the sound box remains in position, or have a remote option triggered by your phone. These updates have made training so much easier. You can take control and can train for this game even when you have no other person present to act as your stooge.

Let's play!

Your dog can reliably go to their bed when the doorbell rings now, so it is time to start building in some delays while you approach the door. With no one waiting at the door, start to step towards it a few paces before returning to reward your dog. Build up the distance between you and your dog so that you can walk to the door and back. Then begin to open the door before returning. In incremental stages, build up the routine you would follow if there really was someone waiting at the door.

Now you are ready for real people to help. Engage helpful family or friends to wait patiently at your door while you work on getting your dog onto their bed and

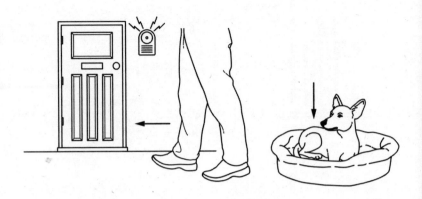

then approach the door. Calmly return to the bed and encourage your dog back on it if they get up too soon. Depending on the excitability of your dog, you may have to work on this stage very slowly, but be patient – it is possible.

When the helper comes in, they should be quiet and calm at first. Rewards can be offered to your dog as the people pass by the bed. Lots of practice will help your dog to succeed with this; it's hard to resist the impulse to rush to say hello.

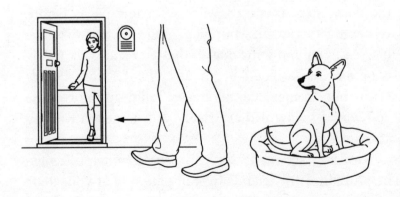

TOP TRAINING TIPS

🐾 This game is great for most dogs but if your dog is genuinely reactive towards guests it is important to ensure that they are always safely elsewhere before you open the door. Discuss the situation with your veterinarian, who can refer you to a behaviour specialist for help.

🐾 Bring on the challenge! Once your dog is getting the hang of the game you can start to build up to more distractions such as people talking, playing about, carrying things in and so on. Lots of temptations that your dog will have to learn to resist. Make it worth their while by rewarding them with their favourite toy if they stay on their bed until the door is closed.

STOP AND GO!

Also known as the 'Red Light, Green Light' game, this activity helps your dog to develop some self-control as they learn that pausing games to pay attention to you is a good idea and doesn't mean that the fun is over forever. The objective is for the dog to move towards you and play when the 'go' or 'green light' cue is given and stop when the 'stop' or 'red light' cue occurs. The goal is for your dog to understand the cues and have sufficient impulse control to respond accordingly. Almost all owners can find a use for this activity, whether at home or while out and about.

WHAT YOU'LL NEED
- Treats
- A toy that encourages your dog to play with you (e.g. a ragger, a flirt pole, or a ball on a rope)

Get ready

Choose an open area, such as your backyard or a large room indoors, where your dog can move freely without obstacles.

Get steady

Ensure that there are no external distractions that will interfere with this game in the early stages.

Let's play!

Start with 'go' or 'green light' training. Begin the game by standing a short distance away from your dog. Ask them to sit or lie down; any static position will work. Use a cheerful tone and say 'go' or 'green light' as an invitation for your dog to come towards you. Encourage this approach by displaying reassuring body language, clapping your hands, or using an enthusiastic voice. You might run backwards, encouraging your dog to follow, or run with your dog beside you; anything to get them to want to be close to you. If your dog prefers toys, then use these to get them to come towards you.

While your dog is approaching or beside you, offer them continuous verbal praise and rewards. This will reinforce their engagement behaviour and motivates them to continue engaging with you.

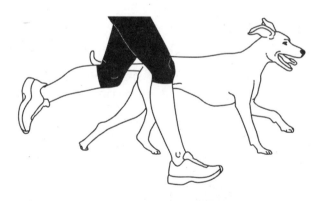

While your dog is still focused on you, clearly say your second cue, 'stop' or 'red light', and immediately stop moving, look at your dog and ask them to 'sit' (or cue another static position). It might take a moment for your dog to recognize that the game has paused, so wait patiently. The game does not progress until they move into the position you have cued. Once they sit, reward

with praise and a treat. Stopping and being still must be a worthwhile response or they won't choose to do it. The game does not progress to 'go' again before your dog has offered the static position.

Now give your 'go' or 'green light' cue and resume the game. Continue alternating between 'go' or 'green light' and the 'stop' or 'red light' cues until your dog's response to the 'stop' becomes faster and more reliable. Ensure that you always heavily reward them for responding.

Increase the difficulty by gradually extending the distance between you and your dog while you play. Vary the length of the go and stop periods to build in duration and focus.

TOP TRAINING TIPS

🐾 Start to add in some distractions while you play. Begin with low-level distraction and build up, perhaps with other people or dogs playing in sight.

🐾 Fancy a group activity? Why don't you encourage your friends with dogs to also teach this game so that you can all play together – a great way to build up more advanced skills and focus! Each dog must follow through and offer the sit or down position before they can go on to the next 'go' stage.

🐾 Bring on the challenge! Full traffic light game. To make the game more engaging, you can introduce variations such as 'amber light' (where games slow down), or even go wild by bringing in 'blue light' (which could be linked to any action, such as spin or jump). These variations add an extra level of fun and mental stimulation for your dog.

CHAPTER 4

LET'S PROBLEM-SOLVE

While your dog may never be a Rubik's Cube champion, there are many other ways that you can develop their problem-solving skills. These activities can be presented first as simple games to encourage their engagement and to build confidence, developing over time into significantly more challenging activities. They help to keep your dog's brain sharp and engaged, while limiting opportunity for mental boredom. A dog with a history of using their brain in this way is more likely to persist with future games and training. As always, the time taken to teach these games is also beneficial for your relationship with them, because of the contact time and your improved awareness of their skills and motivations – and of course because of the necessary rewards and praise they receive when they succeed.

HIDDEN TREAT GAME

WHAT YOU'LL NEED

- 3+ opaque plastic cups
- A container/pouch of dog treats

Get ready

Your dog should already know the action that you want them to perform when they find the hidden treat, so ensure you choose something easy for them to do. For example, a sit or a lie down (see pages 66 and 69).

Decide on your verbal cue to start the game, e.g. 'go find'. You may accompany this with a hand gesture which you will use towards the cups where you will hide the treats

Choose your reward signal: you may be using a clicker, or have a word that you already use to 'mark' or signal to your dog that they have been successful (for more guidance on this see page 41).

Get steady

Begin with one cup and build up the number used as your dog's skills increase. Work on the floor or a surface where your dog can easily reach and sniff. The cups will

be positioned apart at first so that your dog has plenty of space to sniff and so that odour cues from a nearby cup don't confuse them. Try not to handle the treats too much, or all the cups (and anything else you touch) will smell of the treat and could cause confusion.

Let's play!

Encourage your dog to approach the single cup covering a treat and use your verbal cue. Repeatedly allow your dog to approach and sniff the cup, before marking and rewarding every time. Your dog should start to feel very confident approaching the cup and learn that this game is a lot of fun. As they get close and sniff the cup, give your chosen reward signal to indicate that they have done a good job. Then toss another treat from your pouch away from the cup for them to go and eat. Doing

this allows them to naturally reposition and to approach the cup again ready for another go.

Note that we do not feed the treat from under the cup. Doing this could encourage your dog to charge in and knock it over to access the food. This might lead to further problem behaviours when trying to encourage other games. Instead, the performance itself leads to the reward being offered separately, and there is an extra bonus of improved impulse control too.

As you repeat the game, now present a second cup alongside the first, this time with no treat underneath it. If your dog approaches, wait until they are focusing on/ sniffing the cup with the treat before you reward them. Sniffing the empty cup does not warrant a reward: wait patiently until your dog moves to the correct cup and then give your marker signal and toss the reward treat away from the cups. Keep repeating until your dog is confidently approaching the cups and seeking out the one with the hidden treat. Swap their positions about, making sure that you touch both cups between rounds so that each one holds your scent and seems similar.

Now you should introduce your 'I've found it' signal which is the action you taught before starting this game. Return to using just one single cup for this new element to the game. When your dog sniffs the cup hiding the treat, ask them to 'sit' (or give your alternative choice of signal) and then mark and reward as usual. With repetition, this action should start to be offered naturally after your dog notes the scent. Be careful with your timing and only reward if your dog first sniffs and then gives their 'I've found it' signal.

TOP TRAINING TIPS

🐾 If your dog is overly excited by hidden food and cannot contain their enthusiasm, you can work with a scent item instead. Herbal teabags, catnip or vanilla essence on a cotton pad could all be options. These can be used in other games too.

🐾 If your dog is not interested in approaching the cups to begin with, then either position yourself with the cups between you and your dog, or begin with the cup in your hand, held the right way up with the treat/scent inside. Use an excited tone to encourage your dog towards you and to get the game started.

🐾 Bring on the challenge! Once your dog has grasped the concept of the game and can easily find the treat/scent between two cups, add in a third. Make it interesting by positioning the cups further apart, removing your dog from sight before baiting one cup and then bringing them in to work on a fresh arrangement. You might even want to create obstacles or barriers for your dog to work around to get to the cups. Distractions such as toys or people could be introduced for those dogs who are really capable. Can they work despite the temptations?

TOY-BOX CHALLENGE

WHAT YOU'LL NEED
- A few of your dog's favourite toys
- A large box
- A pouch of dog treats

Get ready

Gather a few toys that your dog is already familiar with and enjoys. Each toy will need its own unique name. Choose carefully, as you will need to consistently use this name from now on. It might be a good idea to write these down alongside a description, or photo, of the toy.

In the early stages you will need only a small number of toys, but be prepared to add to these if your dog turns out to be a verbal specialist! Chaser, the famous collie dog, learned to distinguish between 1,022 different toys in her lifetime, so you might end up needing a bigger toy-box ...

Get steady

Introduce each toy individually, allowing your dog to sniff and explore them. As they do, say the toy's name clearly. Then toss a treat away from the toy for your dog to go and eat. As they approach the toy again, repeat its name and once again praise and reward.

Repeat a few times and then put this toy away out of sight. Your dog may require a break from the game, but if they are still keen, move on to the second toy introduction. Repeat the same process with this toy.

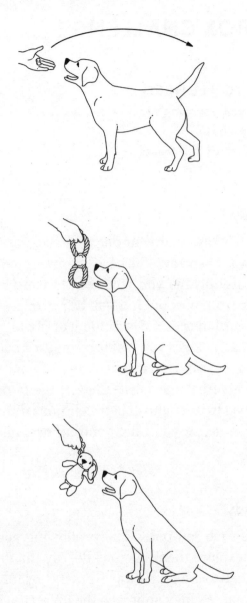

Let's play!

Now your dog knows the name of two toys, you can begin to challenge them to select the correct one by name. Place both toys in front of you, or hold them out, one in each hand, and ask your dog to find one by name.

If your dog approaches the correct toy, reward this choice. If they approach the wrong one, remain still and wait (and resist the desire to help). If they then turn to the correct toy, immediately praise, say the toy's name and reward your dog.

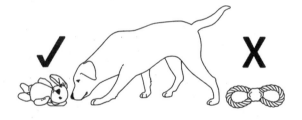

Practise with the toys in different hands, positioned in slightly different ways, and be ready to mark all correct responses. Start to encourage your dog to pick up the toy before you reward them.

TOP TRAINING TIPS

🐾 Once your dog is confidently choosing the correct toy for the majority of your trials, you can bring in additional toys. Start with the new toy alone, saying its name as you did at the start of this game. Then present the new toy along with a previously known one.

🐾 Bring on the challenge! Once your dog is familiar with a range of toys and can pick them out from a line-up, you can build in complexity such as placing them out of your sight so that the decision about which toy to choose is not in some way connected to inadvertent signalling from you.

🐾 There are many subtle signals that handlers give to their animals that can interfere with the learning process. It is well documented that the handler's breathing rate, muscular tension, voice or other micro-movements can accidentally signal to the dog that they have arrived at the correct choice. By placing the toys out of sight (behind furniture or in another room), you remove any such influence.

OUT OF SIGHT BUT NOT OUT OF MIND

WHAT YOU'LL NEED

- 3+ identical opaque tubs, cups or bowls
- A small ball or toy that will fit underneath the containers
- A large towel
- A pouch of treats

Get ready

In this game your dog has to remember where the toy was placed. This is different to a search game because the dog is not using their nose to find the item; rather they are expected to remember where the toy was positioned. The tubs, cups or bowls will be used to hide the ball or toy. Treats can be used, but there is a higher risk that your dog will follow the odour. A dry biscuit and careful handling of the containers can make this possible if your dog is not motivated by toys/items.

You will need a large towel or some other screen to prevent your dog from fixating on one cup or tub. You will need to decide upon what action your dog should take to signal that it's found what it's looking for. This needs to be something easy and known to the dog, such as simply sitting.

Get steady

Position yourself in front of your dog. Show them the toy and then cover it with the tub or cup. Pause. Uncover

the item after a few seconds to show that it still exists.

Repeat and start to ask your dog, 'Where is it?' As they nose at the tub or cup, you can lift it and reveal the hidden toy. They can then either play with the toy, or you can reward them with a treat from your pouch.

Playing a game with the toy each time at the end of this training game will prolong the session considerably, but this might be the necessary motivation for your dog to engage. If they prefer a food reward, it is likely you will be able to fit in more repetitions per session.

You can start to request that your dog performs your chosen action signal before you reveal the hidden toy

and reward them. Over a few sessions repeat this action, very slowly increasing the delay before you reveal the item hidden by the tub. The lesson for your dog here is that while it is not visible, the item continues to exist.

Let's play!

Now place two tubs or cups in front of you. This time let your dog see you place the toy under one of the containers. Pause and ask them, 'Where is it?' Praise and reward as usual when they locate the hidden toy.

Each time you hide the toy you should then touch and lift each of the other tubs. This means that your scent is on them all and your dog is not just learning to go to the only item that was touched by you during that round.

TOP TRAINING TIPS

🐾 To increase the challenge, when the item is hidden under one container, briefly block your dog's sight of the tubs for a second or two and then reveal them again before asking your dog, 'Where is it?' Gradually build up the delay before you reveal what is under the tubs.

🐾 Add in a few more tubs to increase the complexity. Vary which container you hide the toy under.

🐾 Bring on the challenge! You can create a complex game by building up to many tubs under which the toy might be hidden and by prolonging the delay significantly before revealing the options. Start the game and then remove your dog from the room for a short time, engage in another activity and then return to see if your dog still remembers. Perhaps you'll discover that your dog has an eidetic memory!

MORE OR LESS

Did you know that many animals have an awareness of numbers? This is very useful as it allows them to make informed choices, recognize when one of their offspring has been left behind, or work out when one resource is more plentiful than another. Dogs haven't needed to develop skills to do dreaded long division, but they have shown an awareness for numbers and you can explore this with your own dog.

In this game your dog is asked to identify which option has more items than the other. This perception of numerical differences is challenging, so it isn't necessarily a game for beginners. Some dogs will find it easier with food items while others will do well with toys. It depends on your dog's motivations.

WHAT YOU'LL NEED

- Two identical plates
- Portions of dry kibble or treats that can be split into two portions, one larger than the other
- Toys or other objects to demonstrate the principle
- A door gate, or someone to hold your dog's lead

Get ready

Choose your training area, ideally free from distractions and other pets. It helps your dog to understand basic commands if you can get them to sit a short distance away from where you position the plates. If you are unsure whether your dog can do this, clip their lead on and have another person hold them a couple of metres away. Alternatively, you can work with your dog on the other side of a child gate or mesh barrier. Your cues for this game will be 'less' and 'more' (unless you already use these words for another activity).

Get steady

Begin with the simplest concept: one treat on one plate and two on another. Smaller numbers are easier for dogs to understand.

Now, your dog is probably more than happy to charge forwards and eat all the treats on offer. However, the game will soon end and they may have a full belly but no idea of the concept you are trying to teach. Therefore, it is sensible to allow them to move or orientate themselves towards but not to reach either bowl by using a lead or by creating a barrier with a door gate. Remember to praise and reward them with a treat from your pouch.

Let's play!

While your dog is watching, place the plates down onto the floor in front of you, but positioned so that your dog cannot reach them. Allow your dog to see both plates

and then gesture towards the one with 'more' treats. Your dog can be permitted to approach this plate; give your cue word, 'more', as they arrive. Praise and throw them a treat from your pouch.

Reset the game each time by tossing the reward treat behind or to the side so that your dog moves away to eat it. While they do this you can lift the plates and then, once your dog is focusing again, place them down, sometimes swapping their position, other times placing them back down in the same order. Each time, allow your dog to come forwards, and if they are moving to the correct side praise and reward them.

If you wish, you can introduce a 'sit' or 'down' position in front of the plate to act as your dog's signal that this is their answer. This is similar to a sniffer dog signalling they have found something by sitting or pawing at the location. Choose an action that your dog is very familiar with and that indicates no confusion or hesitation. Introduce this action into the game by giving the cue for it once they have approached the correct plate, and then praise and reward once more. Once they have the routine in place, fade out the cue for 'sit'/'down' so that they are not reliant upon you and begin to offer the chosen response themselves when they make their decision.

Gradually add some more treats to the 'more' plate and keep practising. Now let the 'less' plate have some additional food (but not more than the 'more' plate). Can your dog still work it out, or do you notice that it gets harder for them to achieve the right answer as the amounts increase?

TOP TRAINING TIPS

🐾 Repeat and vary the scenarios: practise this exercise with different quantities of treats or toys, gradually increasing the difficulty. Mix up the quantities and the arrangement of the piles to prevent your dog from relying on other cues, such as the physical placement or order.

🐾 Bring on the challenge! Once your dog can play the game with the 'more' cue, teach them to select the 'less' plate on cue instead. Reverse the game and practise giving your 'less' cue and rewarding when they select this one instead.

🐾 If your dog is a maths-whizz you can mix up the choices and practise the game using either cue.

🐾 Practise with different treats, toys or objects to really push their ability further. If you feel creative you can work with cards with different numbers of dots or images for your dog to choose between.

COPY ME

Dogs have been shown to respond well to social learning. Imitation is an area of cognition that has long fascinated researchers trying to understand its role in the animal mind. Copying another animal of the same kind is advantageous, but can dogs observe humans and learn indirectly by watching our actions? Some fascinating research by Claudia Fugazza and her team in Hungary has shown that the 'do as I do' approach can be faster and more effective than the usual associative learning, or even clicker training, for some things. Social learning has rarely been utilized for most forms of training but perhaps now is the time for you to test your dog's ability to learn this way.

WHAT YOU'LL NEED

- A selection of training treats
- Any object you wish to use for the actions (item to touch, pick up, etc.)

Get ready

This training is more complex than for many of the other games in this book since you will need to have taught some established actions already. These choices will vary tremendously; it's a game that can utilize your dog's personal strengths and it will be advantageous for them to already understand the basics and be able to sit and stay in position. To play 'copy me', your dog will need to know a minimum of five established cues that, when performed, look similar to the action and movements you would make yourself if demonstrating them. These could include actions (grab, spin, jump, bow), approaches (going to a specific place or object) and touching of a specific object (targeting with nose, paw, chin, sitting or standing on something). Ideally, the responses should not be natural poses or actions that a dog may do spontaneously, such as sitting, or that bring enjoyment all by themselves, such as playing with a favourite toy. This is to prevent accidental presentation of those behaviours rather than them being the result of imitation. If your dog does not have a range of responses on cue (without any luring or physical guidance), then look through this book for examples and teach those first.

If you are using objects, you should have everything present during all of the training sessions.

Get steady

Establish a starting position in which you place your dog at the start of every repetition. Ideally, this is a position facing you, in an area free from other distractions. Later, once your dog has an understanding of the concept, you will be able to have more freedom in where you play.

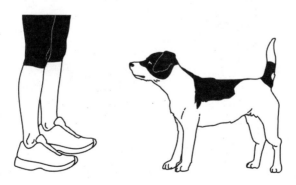

To begin with you will work with three different cues from those known by your dog. Keep the others for later in the training plan. It is important to ensure that the foundation skills for this game are strong, so spend time perfecting them so that your later training is not jeopardized.

Let's play!

Place your dog in the starting position where they will stay. Now, demonstrate your chosen behaviour. If you have moved, return to your starting position and then say 'copy' or 'do it', followed by the verbal cue for the action you have just performed. This might be, 'copy, spin'. Because your dog knows the cue to spin, they should respond with this action. Make sure that you reward them for this correct response. Practise one or two more times, then move on to your next action.

Repeat the same process, starting in the same place each time (this helps to reduce confusion). Demonstrate another chosen response, return to your position and then ask your dog to 'copy', followed by the cue associated with the movement.

Only practise a few times for each action before moving to another in order to prevent your dog from connecting the verbal cue 'copy' with one specific action. The original verbal cue was taught by consistently pairing it with the designated response, so care needs to be taken not to accidentally overwrite this with the new word. By your swapping between responses, your dog should start to learn that the cue 'copy' is guidance to do the action demonstrated to them rather than indicating a specific movement. Gradually introduce a brief pause between the 'copy' and action cue word; observe your dog's behaviour as their response will be a useful indicator of whether they are picking up the rules of this game.

You and your dog are ready to progress to the next

step when they can pre-empt the observed action when you give your 'copy' cue. They no longer need to be told what it is that they should do next as they know it is connected to your previous movement. Remember to always reward your dog when they choose the correct action to replicate.

Hopefully your dog has started to understand the game now. Test them by bringing two or three further actions all at once, mixed among the original three rehearsed responses. Hopefully, your dog will be able to generalize the concept of 'copy' to include these new actions you are demonstrating. If this is successful, well done: you have taught your dog the principles of the game and now can begin to build up their repertoire. If not, don't despair as this is a difficult game and some further practice should help.

As much fun as it is being able to get your dog to copy you, the ultimate outcome of this game is that it can become a way to teach new responses faster and with fewer stages than it would traditionally take. As you add in new actions for your dog to copy, you can assign them their own cue so that eventually they will respond by the cue alone and you won't need to demonstrate first. Do this by getting them to perform the new behaviour until they are doing it reliably. Then you will begin to say your new cue, then 'copy' as they begin. With some practice you will find that your dog starts to respond when you say the new word associated with the action and 'copy' is no longer necessary.

TOP TRAINING TIPS

🐾 If this is working well you can now begin to change locations and build in some more distractions.
Be prepared to practise and to think carefully about your actions and how you cue your dog to respond. Taking your time and getting the skills established at each stage will pay off in the long term.

🐾 Your imagination rules in this game. You can bring in as many actions, simple or complex, as you can think of. The only rule is that it must be something your dog is physically capable of doing without risk.

🐾 Bring on the challenge! Why not try to build in some more complex responses? If you haven't already taught actions like opening the cupboard or getting the lead, you could try to create these responses by demonstrating and requesting them to 'copy'.

ROVER READS

Although very clever, your dog will never appreciate literary masterpieces. Despite this, it is possible for them to associate visual cues with specific actions. This can be a brilliant cognitive challenge while also being very impressive for those observing.

WHAT YOU'LL NEED
- Treats
- Cards with printed or drawn symbols

Get ready

Before involving your dog, you should choose which visual cues you will use for this game. Think of some actions your dog knows well that could be suited to this game: spin, paw, down etc. Each of these will need their own unique image or symbol. Large cards for them are ideal. To make these durable during training, they can be laminated or placed in plastic pockets.

Get steady

Move to a quiet location with few distractions. Practise a few known actions and offer rewards to get your dog into the mood for learning.

Let's play!

Begin with one symbol and action at a time. You will need to associate the symbol with the action by pairing them together.

Stand in front of your dog and get their attention. Show your dog the symbol and then immediately perform the associated action. For instance, show the symbol for 'spin' and then ask your dog to spin by giving your usual, previously taught cue (verbal or hand signal). Repeat this process several times, consistently using the symbol and the cue for the associated action together. Each time your dog successfully performs the action after seeing the symbol, reward them with treats and praise. This will help to reinforce the association between the symbol and the action.

After a number of repetitions you can test your dog's understanding. Present them with the symbol without giving the verbal command. Wait to see if they perform the correct action based on the visual cue alone. If so, reward and reinforce this behaviour.

Over time, one by one, introduce further symbols and work on associating these with the chosen actions. Repeat the process of showing the symbol and asking your dog to perform the corresponding action, reinforcing and rewarding correct responses until your dog is highly proficient.

TOP TRAINING TIPS

🐾 Begin to practise in different environments, with some distractions and with other people present.

🐾 Bring on the challenge! You can build up a range of symbols for the activities your dog knows. You could even connect certain symbols with specific toys. A twist on the game would be to present the cards to your dog and allow them to choose which toy you get out to play with. The options are endless, so have fun!

PUPICURE

Teaching your dog to file their own nails on a scratchboard is a great solution to the common problem of being uncomfortable with nail clippers or a Dremel tool. Teaching this game is both mentally stimulating as well as providing physical benefits. This game is almost a two-part process, with the front and back feet taking different approaches. This is a great opportunity for your dog to cooperate with their nail-care regime.

WHAT YOU'LL NEED

- Treats
- File board: you can purchase a ready-made board from various suppliers, or create your own
- A dust cloth or flannel

Get ready

Prepare your file board. If you are making one yourself, take care to ensure that the edges of the sandpaper go around the end of the board or pipe and that there are no overlapping sections. This is to prevent your dog's nails catching and ripping the sheets off. Use a non-toxic adhesive, making sure it's secure before allowing your dog to use it.

If your dog has already learned the 'wipe your feet' game, they will probably be quick to advance with this game. Knowing how to 'step up' (page 240) will be an advantage for the hind-feet training section.

Get steady

Your first task is to teach your dog to put their paws onto the board. They need to be very comfortable with this stage before progressing. Lay the board flat on the floor and praise and reward your dog each time they approach and explore it, and then for each time they put their paws on it. Toss the treat away from the board so that your dog has the chance to reset their position and come back towards the board repeatedly.

Let's play!

Front-paw training

Once your dog is confidently approaching the board, raise one end of it slightly and encourage them to come and put their paws on it. Ensure it is stable. If your dog is happy to stand on the board but not inclined to swipe it with their feet, try raising it to a more vertical position. Lower the angle if your dog is struggling to contact it at all.

Ensure that your reward marker, 'yes' or click occurs as soon as your dog makes contact with the board with a foot. Offer the treat while your dog is in position on the board. The position of the board makes it more likely that the swiping motion will occur.

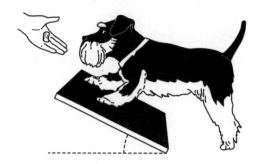

Now add in your cue word, 'scratch', while your dog uses a swipe or digging action on the board. Always praise and reward them with a treat for successful actions. Some dogs will use one foot at a time, others will use both feet together. Each dog has their own style.

For cases when the dog needs some encouragement to scratch more enthusiastically, you may wish to try a slightly different approach. Start with the board flat on the floor. Hide a treat behind a cloth laid out on the board; you may need to hold the material tightly against angled boards to prevent the treat from immediately rolling out. Your dog will have to scrape with their foot to access the treat; as they make a swiping motion the idea is that they are able to gain access to the treat so if you are holding the material, loosen it at this point. Repeat by hiding another treat behind the cloth and allow your dog to scrabble at it again to access the treat.

Take each step slowly. Elevate the board slowly over time to encourage more natural scratching. The more vertical positions work well to create the correct angle for the nail to be filed rather than the pad. Explore positional options to see what works best for your size of dog; prop the board up against a wall or piece of furniture, or even against the back of a chair if your dog can stand comfortably on the seat area. Whatever position you select, make sure it's secure and won't slip when your dog uses it.

The great aspect of this game is that every time you practise with your dog, even before they are fully trained in it, it is helping their nails to remain short. Remove the board between sessions so that your dog cannot access it unintentionally.

Back-paw training

Getting the position right is vital for success in this part of the lesson. Many dogs are not particularly aware of their back feet and so it often takes longer to train this part. It can be helpful to set up a place for your dog to 'step up', since this makes it easier for the back feet to be raised.

Lean the scratching board so that it sits angled against the step, or stairs, you are using. Ask your dog to place their front feet up on the step beyond the board so that it is underneath them and between their front and back legs. Use a treat to lure them to stretch themselves up

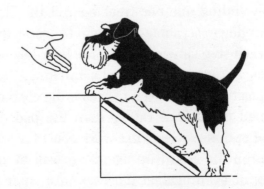

further; doing this usually means that they raise one rear foot off the floor. Immediately mark this action with a 'yes' or click and follow up with the treat. Continue to encourage this paw to raise and to eventually make contact with the board. Each dog will have a slightly different position that makes this possible, so observe them and how they are moving, and adapt to encourage success.

TOP TRAINING TIPS

🐾 Regularly check your dog's nails. This method of filing can make a big difference in a short time, so check often that the nails are not getting too short or that the quick (the sensitive part of the nail) is not being exposed. If you see any issues, stop using the scratch board and consult your vet.

🐾 While this method can be a great way to maintain your dog's nails, it may not completely replace the need for clipping or grinding, especially for dogs with very thick nails. Always consult with your vet or a professional groomer if you're unsure.

🐾 Bring on the challenge! While this game is sufficiently tricky as it is, it might be useful for your dog to be able to work with different family members so that nail-care duties are divided. However, make sure to check before playing, to avoid any risk of over-filing if multiple people are involved.

STRING PULL

Teaching your dog to pull on a string attached to a treat can be a fun and interactive game, and advanced versions have been used in cognitive studies comparing the domestic dog with wolves. The challenge presented to those canines in the study was to choose the string attached to the treat, and to ignore the one that was not connected, demonstrating an awareness of environmental consequences and problem-solving ability. Dogs were outperformed by wolves in that study, but perhaps your dog can be a champion for their kind.

WHAT YOU'LL NEED
- Ribbon or hessian jute string (the length depends on your dog, but it should be 30–50 cm long at a minimum)
- Treats (large enough to attach the string to them)
- A door gate, or alternative barrier, to limit access to the treats

Get ready

Find a quiet and secure area indoors or outdoors where you can conduct the training without distractions.

Get steady

Show your dog the string and let them sniff and investigate it. Encourage their curiosity by moving the string around gently. Some dogs will prefer to get started by tugging on a string held in your hand, others

will naturally swipe it on the floor with their paws; for this game it doesn't matter as long as they are pulling it towards themselves. Hold a treat close to your dog's nose to grab their attention. Slowly slide the treat along the string, allowing them to follow it with their eyes and paws. This should encourage contact with the string, which might otherwise be an irrelevant item in your dog's opinion.

Let's play!

Place your dog on the other side of a doorgate, or alternative barrier. Attach a treat to one end of the string by loosely tying a knot around it, or by pushing the treat between the weave of the string. Allow your dog to see you doing this. The string can now be positioned so that the treat end is on the far side of the barrier and your dog can only reach the unattached end.

When your dog shows interest in the string or makes an attempt to touch it or pull on it, encourage them by using your verbal marker, 'yes', or a clicker to mark the behaviour, followed by a treat reward. This helps your dog understand that pulling on the string is a desirable action.

Once your dog starts to show consistent interest in the string and makes attempts to pull on it, add a verbal cue such as 'pull' or 'tug'. Watch your dog carefully, and just as they move to engage with the string, use your cue, and follow it with the verbal marker or clicker and a treat reward.

Gradually increase the difficulty for your dog. You can do this by holding your end of the string slightly tighter, offering more resistance as your dog pulls. This encourages them to use more strength and

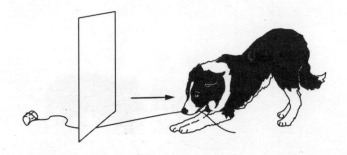

determination, which will help them to obtain the treat. Each time your dog successfully pulls on the string, use the cue, mark the behaviour, and reward them.

As your dog becomes more comfortable and proficient at pulling on the string, shape the behaviour by rewarding stronger and more intentional pulls. You can also increase the distance between your dog and the treat to challenge them further.

Once your dog consistently pulls on the string to retrieve the treat, gradually increase the duration of the pulling action, waiting until the string has been pulled through before marking the action and rewarding your dog.

Now add in another string. This one should not be attached to a treat. Lie it across the barrier in the same way as with the first string so that your dog can see which one has the treat and which one does not. Distance these apart so that your dog has to deliberately choose between the strings. If they pull the string that is not attached to the treat, there will be no rewards forthcoming. Your dog must learn the difference in what they can see.

To increase the choice for your dog, you can build up to having several strings available for them to pull.

This game requires supervision since it is important that the string or ribbon is not ingested along with the treat.

TOP TRAINING TIP

🐾 Bring on the challenge! Let's recreate the research set-up used when they compared dogs with wolves. Set out two strings across the barrier for your dog to observe. One is tied to the treat, the other is not attached but there is a treat positioned an inch or so from the end of it. Your dog will have to pay attention to which string is going to drag the treat towards them. Which will they choose? They need to experience the frustration of pulling on an unattached string, and its corresponding lack of rewards, to learn about the concept – so allow them to explore. Over time, will they start to choose the one tied to the treat? In research, domestic dogs (albeit those living freely in a group rather than in homes) weren't particularly skilled at making this deduction. Perhaps your dog will stand out from the rest.

CHAPTER 5

LET'S PERFORM

Teaching your dog to perform tricks offers myriad benefits that have far-reaching implications beyond the obvious 'entertainment' factor. As previously discussed, all fun training can enhance the bond between you and foster trust and cooperation that can reach into other areas, including husbandry and general routines. Trick training is a quick and easy way to keep the brain engaged and can keep the dog moving. Some of the tricks can help during health examinations too, by helping to get the dog into position to be checked. Being successful in these games can boost confidence while they master new skills and receive more praise and rewards. And if you simply love showing off your clever dog to family and friends, that's fine too.

ROLL OVER, ROLL OVER

WHAT YOU'LL NEED
- A selection of small treats
- A comfortable place for your dog to lie and roll

Get ready

Choose a non-distracting environment, free from other animals and one in which your dog is sufficiently relaxed to lie down and focus on the training. It is very useful for your dog to already know how to lie 'down' as a foundation skill for this trick.

Get steady

Get your dog's attention and ask them to move into a down position ready to begin.

The rolling motion can be shaped by holding a treat close to your dog's nose and luring their head around towards their shoulder. As they turn their head it is natural for them to shift their weight over onto the opposite side of the body. The hand movement involved in luring will eventually become your hand gesture for the roll over action.

You might find that your dog only tilts their head slightly at first. Don't worry – you can encourage them by rewarding for gradual approximations of the desired movement: first rewarding as they turn their head, then when they shift their body, then as they follow the treat further around, and finally when they roll over onto their back.

Let's play!

Now that you can get your dog to roll over with the lure, you can progress.

As they shift their weight to roll over, say your cue, 'roll over', and release the treat. Remember to be quick to reward them for the desired behaviour so that they are

keen to try again. Your hand gesture can start to fade out now that your dog is accustomed to the movement. Try to get them to roll over without you holding a treat in your hand (as you encouraged them to before), but be ready to say your cue and reward them when they succeed.

With practice you can phase out the big hand gesture and make it into a more discreet arcing movement accompanying your verbal cue.

TOP TRAINING TIPS

🐾 Be mindful of your position while you teach this lesson. Keep your arm bent so that your elbow is out of your dog's way when they try to roll. Go slowly and allow time for them to shift their body weight.

🐾 Bring on the challenge! Now move the lesson to new locations, always remembering to praise and reward. If your dog is keen, you can chain two or three roll-overs together for a more spectacular response.

🐾 Can you teach your dog to roll the opposite way now? Start again and use a different cue and you'll soon have the option. If you would like a more practical outcome from this trick, you can teach your dog to roll only halfway, before pausing so that they are on their backs. This position makes it easier for the vet to check their undercarriage for wounds or post-surgery.

FAINTING FIDO

WHAT YOU'LL NEED
- A selection of treats

Get ready

In preparation for this trick you should ensure that your dog has already learned a reliable response to 'sit' and 'down' cues. These will serve as building blocks for this response.

Decide on the verbal cue that you will use in this lesson, e.g. 'faint' or 'drama'.

Choose your reward signal: you may be using a clicker, or have a word that you already use to 'mark' or signal to your dog that they have been successful (for more guidance on this see page 41).

Get steady

Begin in a quiet area where your dog is comfortable lying down. Some dogs prefer a rug or carpet to do this trick on.

Let's play!

Ask your dog to lie in the down position to start. Before you begin, pay attention to how your dog is lying. If they are over on one hip, this will guide you to train them to roll over onto this side, since they are part way there already.

Using a treat in one hand, hold this to your dog's nose and lure them by moving it in an arc around their shoulder opposite to the side where they are lying over on one hip. As their head turns to follow the treat, you will notice that their opposite shoulder will dip and they will naturally roll onto their side.

If your dog does not roll over onto their side immediately, don't worry. Some dogs need to be carefully shaped into this position. Lure them to turn their head around towards their shoulder and reward. Then repeat, pulling the treat just a fraction further before allowing them to eat it. Gradually your dog will start to move their head further around, which will

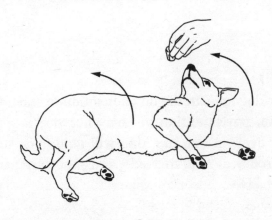

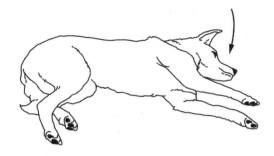

naturally encourage them to eventually manoeuvre into position. Reward all incremental progress until they are fully on their side before the reward is offered. This might happen very quickly, or take a few sessions.

Success with this sort of game often depends on how comfortable your dog is, whether they have any aches and pains, and how relaxed they are in this environment; even the shape of their body can help or hinder the movement. Take your time and you will get there.

Once your dog is rolling onto their side, you can start to move the treat so that their head is flat on the floor before you release it.

Now you are ready to bring in your verbal cue. Use this cue consistently, timing it to coincide with the moment your dog is in the desired position each time. Repetition and consistency will help your dog associate the verbal cue with the behaviour.

The hand and arm movement you have been making as you lure your dog over will now become your cue for the response. You will no longer have to hold a treat in your hand, and will instead reward your dog from your pouch once they have completed the action.

Now that your dog is able to roll over onto their side

easily, you can start to subtly change this from the full lure movement to a smaller arc, eventually minimising it so much that perhaps you will only need to use a finger gesture to trigger the action. Accompany your 'faint' cue with this gesture simultaneously to create a strong association.

TOP TRAINING TIPS

🐾 Practise and repeat this game over several short training sessions lasting a few minutes until your dog can move into position quickly upon hearing/seeing the cue.

🐾 Bring on the challenge! Now work to generalize this response by practising in different rooms, outside, and around various distractions. Soon your dog will be ready to swoon for an audience.

TELL ME A SECRET

Choose a quiet and calm location to begin where you and your dog can focus without distractions. It's best to start the training indoors before moving to more distracting environments.

WHAT YOU'LL NEED
- Some treats

Get ready

If your dog has already learned to target touch with their nose, this game will be super-fast. If not, don't fret since it is easy to teach.

Get steady

Hold a treat between your index and middle finger, ready to lure your dog into position.

You will need to crouch or sit on the floor so that your dog can reach your ear.

Let's play!

Bring your fingers holding the treat up close to your ear. Allow your dog to follow it and when they are very close you can praise them and release the treat.

Repeat until your dog is able to follow your hand up to your ear quickly. Start to say the cue, 'secret', as your dog is moving towards your ear and remember to treat and praise for the right response.

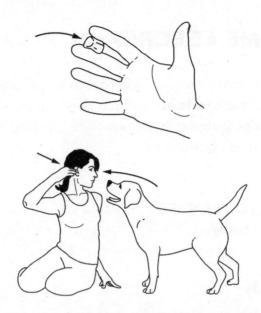

Now you should fade out the treat by pointing to your ear without a treat. When your dog follows your hand and contacts your ear, you should praise and offer a reward from your other hand.

Prolong the contact with your ear by pausing a moment before praising and rewarding. Gradually build up until your dog can hold the position for several seconds.

TOP TRAINING TIPS

🐾 Bring on the challenge! You can fade the pointing gesture to your ear by moving your hand towards your ear but not right up to it and waiting for your dog to make contact before praising and rewarding. You can work up to having no hand gesture at all, just the verbal cue, 'secret'.

LOOK LEFT AND LOOK RIGHT

WHAT YOU'LL NEED
- Some training treats

Get ready

Begin in an area where your dog is relaxed and not distracted. Encourage them to come and sit in front of you.

Get steady

Hold a treat in your right hand. Remember that in this game, when you use your right hand your dog is actually going to look to their left when they are facing you. Try not to confuse your cues during the game.

Let's play!

Show your dog the treat in your right hand and move it slowly outwards to your right side, at dog-head height. Your dog is likely to follow the treat and turn their head to their left. Mark this movement with a click or a 'yes' and offer them the treat.

Repeat this several times until your dog consistently and without hesitation follows the treat with their gaze.

Now you can add in your verbal cue. As your dog turns their head to their left you say 'look left'. Now reward with the treat and praise.

Over a few short sessions continue to practise pairing the action with the verbal cue. Removing the lure comes

next, so begin to move your hand out to the side without holding a treat as a lure. Immediately respond to correct responses by your dog by praising and offering them a treat from your pouch.

Teaching the 'look right' action uses the same approach but with your left hand drawing your dog's focus over towards their right side. Repeat until this movement is fast and reliable. Then add in your 'look right' cue and practise as you did before.

Focus on saying your verbal cue a moment before you give your hand signal to the side. If your dog is recognizing the cue they will begin to respond by turning

their head to the appropriate side. Always remember to praise and reward correct actions.

Fade out your hand signal. Rather than reaching right out to one side or another you can change this hand movement to a small point, or even no physical movement at all, just the verbal cue. Practise asking 'look left' with the full hand signal to your right. Then repeat with a smaller hand gesture, gradually moving your hand less and less over subsequent repetitions. Reward all correct responses with a treat from your pouch.

If at any time your dog gets confused and struggles, go back to an easier step and make the changes more gradually.

TOP TRAINING TIPS

Practise in different areas, with increasing amounts of distraction.

Bring on the challenge! Build this game into your street walks, asking your dog to stop at the kerb, look left, look right, before crossing over. While your dog may not know this is useful for traffic awareness, doing this routinely might help them to pause before crossing a road and could reduce risks.

CROSS-OVER

This game teaches your dog to lie down and cross their legs – a very cute pose, and perfect for photos.

WHAT YOU'LL NEED
- A selection of treats
- A comfortable place for your dog to lie down

Get ready

The basic staple of this game is the down position, so work on this if your dog is not already able to do this competently. The second useful technique is to give a paw; if your dog can already do this, you are well prepared for the game.

Get steady

Encourage your dog into a down position in front of you. You should be crouched or seated on the floor in front of your dog. Ask them to give you a paw while holding your hand out next to one foot. If they respond, then praise and treat. If not, it's probably time to go back and work on getting a 'paw' response before continuing.

While this game appears to be great for less active dogs, please be careful if your dog has any problems with their shoulders or front legs. If your lovely dog is blessed with short legs, this might not be the easiest game for them; assess what they can physically do and devise your own version of the game or focus on another lesson.

Let's play!

To progress, ask your dog to give you their paw, but move your hand slightly over the other one. Reward them immediately for responding. Gradually practise, drawing that paw further over the other.

Start to lower your hand so that it is resting on the opposite leg when you request they give 'paw'. This familiarizes them with the contact, ready for the next step.

Say 'cross-over paw' as you put your hand out. This will link the cue 'cross-over' with the act of giving the paw. Repeat the practice and eventually you will find that your dog starts to respond to the verbal cue, 'cross-over', alone.

Progress to putting out your hand to request the paw

but withdraw it slightly so that your dog's paw rests on their own leg. Immediately reward them to capture this action. Repeat until this cross-legged action is occurring each time and reward on every successful occasion.

Start to fade out your hand gesture so that your dog responds and crosses over their paw without your hand being particularly close. Continue to offer praise throughout.

TOP TRAINING TIPS

🐾 Observe your dog before you begin so that you have an idea about which paw they prefer to use first. This will be the best one to start the game with.

🐾 Bring on the challenge! Once you have taught cross-over one way, you can start to work on teaching it the other way too. Use the same approach to teach your dog to uncross their legs on cue, likewise.

AW, SHUCKS!

This cute trick is fun to teach and looks adorable too. Teaching a dog to 'be shy' typically means training them to perform an action that mimics shyness, such as putting their paw over their face. Of course, we are not trying to create a shy emotion in any way and your dog should enjoy this game as long as it is taught using positive reinforcement.

WHAT YOU'LL NEED
- A surface your dog is comfortable lying on
- Treats for rewarding your dog
- Sticky notes

Get ready

Choose a quiet area in your home where you can conduct the training session without distractions. Make sure it's a place where your dog feels safe and relaxed. Select a verbal cue that will act as a signal to your dog to perform the movement, such as 'be shy'. Use this cue consistently throughout the training process to help your dog associate it with the desired behaviour.

Cut a small piece from a sticky note, just large enough to stick on your dog's nose.

Get steady

Begin with your dog in a sitting position, as this makes it easier for them to perform the desired action.

Ensure from the start that your dog is comfortable around the sticky note and is not worried by it. Do this by holding it in your hand and letting your dog sniff and explore it. Gently touch your dog's nose with the sticky note, not allowing it to stick on just yet. Immediately praise and reward them with a treat. Try a couple more times, hopefully seeing your dog remain calm and comfortable each time.

Let's play!

Now, gently stick the note on the top of your dog's muzzle behind their nose. Your dog might try to remove the note using their paw, which is exactly what you want, so be ready to reward them with a treat and praise. If they try other methods (like rubbing their nose on a surface), don't reward that behaviour. Even if the paw only comes

up towards the nose, this is worth reinforcing as you can gradually work towards closer contact and a fuller swipe on the nose. Repeat a few times until your dog is proficiently bringing their paw up over their muzzle.

As your dog raises their paw over their muzzle is a perfect time to add in your verbal cue, 'be shy'. Reward them after they have completed the action.

Progress to using smaller pieces of the sticky note, gradually reducing the size over multiple training sessions. Continue to use your verbal cue and rewards for each success. Eventually, your dog should start to respond to the cue without the sticky note being necessary.

Start to pause before marking and praising the paw-over-nose response, in order to prolong it slightly. Do this very gradually, so that the duration of the response is slowly increased.

TOP TRAINING TIPS

🐾 Your dog is likely to favour one paw over the other. Once you have worked to perfect the game with one, why not try to shape the action with the other? It might take time and a lot more shaping, but it is possible.

🐾 Bring on the challenge! If your dog has the physical ability and strength to sit up on their haunches, you can work on teaching them to cover up their eyes with both paws together.

MAKE A WISH

Tricks like this may be cute to watch, but more importantly, every time you work on teaching something new to your dog they are stimulated mentally and have the bonus of quality time with you.

WHAT YOU'LL NEED

- Some treats to reward your dog
- Depending on the size of your dog, a chair or stool that they can comfortably reach with their front paws

Get ready

This trick is easier for dogs that already have some training basics such as 'sit' and 'paw'.

Ask your dog to sit close to the chair or alternative platform you have chosen for this game.

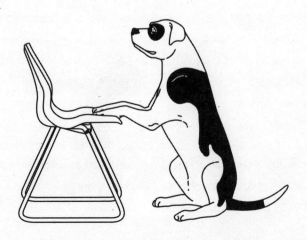

Get steady

The first stage is to encourage your dog into position with their front paws on the chair. You might have to lure them with a treat to do this. If their hindquarters rise off the floor, lower the treat slightly so that they sink down again while their front paws remain on the chair. Reward and praise your dog as they get into this position. Practise this position until they are very comfortable doing this first part.

Let's play!

With your dog in position, paws on the chair, take a treat in one hand and reach underneath their front legs so that the treat is offered between their front legs. They should dip their head down to take this. Repeat until they find it easy to dip their head between their front legs in this manner.

You can start to give your verbal cue at this stage. 'Make a wish' can be said just as your dog moves into position with their nose between their legs. Now your

dog is in the 'making a wish' position, so ensure you mark this with a 'yes' or a click and reward your dog.

With practice your dog will become increasingly comfortable with this trick and so you will be able to fade out your treat lure. Begin, initially, to use the luring gesture without the treat, then mark and reward with a treat from your other hand afterwards. Next, start to reduce the hand movement slightly, over many repetitions. Your dog should be learning to associate the cue phrase with the action more and more as you practise, and this should eventually be sufficient to trigger the movement by itself. Always reward your dog afterwards.

TOP TRAINING TIP

🐾 Bring on the challenge! Build up the duration of this trick gradually. It can be difficult, at first, for a dog that is not used to this position, so take it slowly and, initially, pause only briefly before rewarding them. Gradually increase the duration of the position as they become more proficient.

BELLY TIME!

This game is ideal for dogs who are already comfortable rolling over and having their belly scratched. It's important to note that dogs who roll over submissively may not enjoy being touched in this position, so be mindful of their comfort level. Focus on building your dog's confidence and teach this game in a relaxed location where they feel at ease.

WHAT YOU'LL NEED
- Some training treats
- A comfortable place for your dog to lie down

Get ready

If you haven't taught 'roll over' (page 202) then this is a great place to begin. Otherwise, you can capture natural behaviour when your dog is feeling playful and rolls over showing their belly, by saying a cue such as 'belly time' and ensuring to reward them well. Take care to look at all the signalling so that you are confident you are not mistaking an appeasing gesture for an invitation to pet.

Get steady

Get your dog into a down position in an area free from distractions.

Let's play!

Hold a treat near to your dog's nose, allowing them

to sniff it. As you have done before with the roll-over cue, slowly move your hand around to their shoulder, prompting them to turn their head and follow the treat. If you do this at a slow pace, your dog should naturally shift their weight onto their shoulder, which is the first step. Reward them with a treat once they achieve this stage.

Repeat the process until your dog feels comfortable shifting over onto their side, then lure them a little further, encouraging them to roll onto their back. Once your dog is lying belly-up, immediately praise them and offer a reward before they continue over to the other side in the full 'roll over' position.

Repeat and begin to add in your cue, 'belly time', as they roll over. Eventually you will be able to fade the lure and start to make your hand gestures smaller.

Build up the duration of the belly-up position by pausing before releasing a treat each time.

TOP TRAINING TIPS

🐾 Teaching your dog to show their belly makes it easier and less stressful when they need to be examined by you or your vet, as they already associate the movement with rewards and petting. This is preferable to forcing them onto their back. It can also be useful during grooming sessions.

🐾 Bring on the challenge! You can introduce variations of this game by holding the treat further from your dog's nose once they are lying on their backs to encourage them to reach out with their paws. This would be a nice addition to the yoga dog activity (page 246).

CHAPTER 6

LET'S STAY YOUNG AT HEART

The games in this section can be played by dogs of all ages, of course, but they are particularly suitable for older dogs that are newer to training, or with a simpler skill set, or those that might need activities that are gentler on the joints and muscles.

Why should your older dog be encouraged to play? Keeping the body moving through the various life stages, even through gentle exercise, slows the impact of ageing on cognitive ability. Providing mental stimulation and encouraging continued learning protects the brain even further. It is imperative to tailor activities for your individual dog as they age, since the range of capabilities will be wide. You might have an ageing dog that has a lifetime's experience of training with you – in this case, you can continue to train but with modifications to protect against injury and to account for changing sensory systems. If the dog is advanced in years, but has limited training and activity experience, build it into their routine slowly and within their capability. This will avoid frustrations and maximize enjoyment.

Older dogs may have tighter calorie limitations than younger dogs, or may have developed sensitive digestions. Consider this when setting up any game and work within their comfortable range.

SCATTER FEEDING FUN

WHAT YOU'LL NEED
- A portion of your dog's dry food, or small treats
- A clear floor surface

Get ready

Prepare an area where your dog can safely move about with their nose to the ground. If your dog has vision problems, ensure this area is hazard-free and ideally allow them to become accustomed to the space in their own time.

Get steady

Using an excited voice and playful manner, encourage your dog to engage. If they need some motivation, you can show them the food and feed them one piece to build enthusiasm. Progressing to throwing one piece down to the floor near their feet gets them thinking about looking for food at floor level. Your dog may be new to this idea, or a complete pro, so go at their pace.

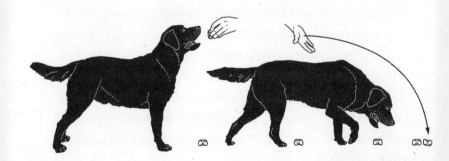

Let's play!

Scatter the treats on the floor and encourage your dog to 'go find'. They will have to move about nose to floor to find and consume their meal. This extends the time required and encourages more movement than the typical routine of eating from a bowl.

TOP TRAINING TIPS

🐾 Begin with small amounts of food fairly close to your dog. As they become proficient at the game you can begin to scatter over a wider area, increasing the difficulty level and the distance your dog has to search.

🐾 The senses start to decline with age, so for some dogs, their sense of smell will be less sensitive than in their earlier years. These dogs might require a stronger-smelling food item, or to see you scattering or laying a trail in order to understand the opportunity being set for them.

🐾 Bring on the challenge! If your dog is enthusiastic about searching for every last piece, you can scatter the food on grass if you are playing outside, around (or on) obstacles, or over specifically designed snuffle mats. You can increase the area, create trails with the food and even scatter it while your dog is not present to observe. Work on a game that suits your dog's sensory capacities; for some this game is a carefully controlled food-dispensing game, while for others it will more resemble a food explosion!

CHIN REST

WHAT YOU'LL NEED
- Some of your dog's training treats
- Small towel/cushion
- A stool/chair or higher surface suitable for your dog to rest their chin on as you advance your training

Get ready

The aim is to teach your dog to press their chin into your hand. To begin with you are aiming to get your dog interested in moving towards you. Do this by holding out a treat and encouraging your dog to approach and take it. Repeat while standing in different places around your home. Most dogs are confident to do this stage, but if you have a dog that is more wary, take your time to encourage a really confident approach before moving on.

Get steady

Now, when your dog approaches to take the treat, hold your other hand with the palm facing upwards, underneath the hand holding the treat. Ensure that you position your hands so that they are approximately head height for your dog. It may be too difficult for them to have to reach up, or stoop low. When they take the treat their face will naturally move over the palm of your other hand. At this stage the chin does not have to make contact; you are just getting your dog accustomed to approaching the flat hand.

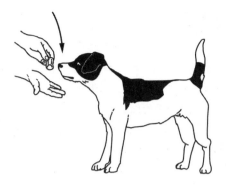

Let's play!

Now we will encourage contact between the chin and your palm. Hold your palm out flat and encourage your dog to approach to take the treat from your other hand as usual. As your dog moves to take the treat, lower it so that their chin naturally contacts your flat palm as they eat. When contact is made between the chin and your hand, you can praise, or use your marker word, 'yes'. (While clicker training is possible for this, it is not advisable to click while your dog's head is so close to your hand/the clicker. A marker word or praise is usually enough to get this game started.)

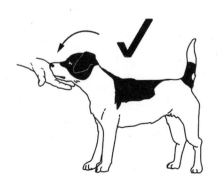

Repeat until your dog is comfortable approaching and dipping their head onto your palm as they take the treat. Make sure that they make full contact with your hand before you release the treat.

Now you have the action occurring reliably, you can add in your cue word, 'touch' or 'chin', as they make contact. This will now be the cue that you use to elicit this specific response. After a few repetitions start to say it a moment before they make contact and then reward once the chin rests on your palm.

Introduce pausing for a second, then two, three ... before releasing the treat to prolong the contact.

Now start to hold out your palm without the treat being held directly above it. Initially it will help to have the treat in your other hand but held close to your body so that it remains discreet and doesn't distract your dog, while allowing you to swiftly reward the correct response when it occurs.

Practise until you can say 'touch' or 'chin' just before presenting your hand and when this triggers your dog to approach and make contact. Reward them consistently for firm contact.

Be patient and wait for your dog to think the activity through before prompting again.

Begin to practise in different locations around your home and while you are sitting and standing; obviously, if you have a tiny dog, then bending over to do this frequently will be awkward, so make sure you are comfortable. Small dogs might benefit from doing this while on a table (make sure it's non-slip and that they cannot accidentally jump or fall off) or beside you on a chair. This can be great practice for times when they are checked on a table at a veterinary clinic.

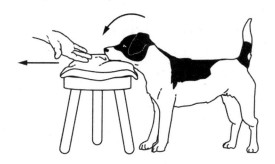

To progress your training, you can transfer your dog's chin contact onto a folded towel or small cushion so that in the future you can encourage them to target this, freeing up both hands to groom, check your dog over, administer medicines and so on.

Fold up your towel into a small pad and set it on your knee or onto a surface that your dog can easily rest their chin on. Depending on the size of your dog, this might be placed on a footstool, chair, or even a table for those of you with very large dogs.

Hold your upward palm over the towel and encourage the contact as before. Reward your dog well for doing this in the new position.

Now, as your dog moves to rest on your palm, move your hand back at the last moment so that they contact the towel instead; immediately offer the reward. Repeat until your dog is coming and resting their chin onto this location instead of your hand.

Remember that when you want to release your dog from a position, you can use your 'All done' cue as discussed on page 42. It can be useful as a cue telling your dog that the activity is over and they can move away.

TOP TRAINING TIPS

🐾 If you need to increase your dog's enthusiasm, you can take some quick steps backwards as they move towards you. This will bring energy into the game and encourage them to close the distance.

🐾 Bring on the challenge! Start to build up to longer durations and with distractions. If you practise often enough, you can even do this while another family member gently builds in brushing or examinations. Keep these very brief at first, just a few seconds at a time, and build up the sustained position until your dog can reliably follow a chin-rest cue.

🐾 Move on to introducing this game in a quiet veterinary waiting room. Once your dog can do this, you can encourage them to do it briefly in the examination room. Don't try to insist on them doing so while they are checked by your veterinarian until you have built up to this stage, but ultimately this is a goal you can aim for.

SNIFFY WALKS

WHAT YOU'LL NEED

- Just you and your dog on a lead and plenty of time and patience

Get ready

The aim of this game is to allow your dog to fully enjoy the world of smells in their own time. So, for this game it is important that you are in no rush. You might want to choose a walking location that is interesting for you, but whether you are ambling along a woodland path or taking a walk around the neighbourhood, the rule is that you go at your dog's pace. Clear your schedule and wear suitable clothing so that you can stroll alongside your dog.

Get steady

If your dog is still pretty active, you might want to introduce this routine for walks in appropriate areas, or at a certain part of your walk where you encourage them to 'go sniff'. For older dogs, who are naturally slower, possibly experiencing some changes due to joint discomfort, the entire walk might be a sniffy one. It may be that you only make it down one street or path: the distance does not matter as long as your dog is sniffing and exploring the world around them (safely on a lead if you are near roads, of course).

Let's play!

You might need to accept a mental shift for this activity. Most of us are used to a certain pace of walking and to encouraging our dogs to keep up.

Older dogs that can no longer run and play with their canine companions can feel thoroughly happy after a slow, sniffy walk (or 'sniffari') around their neighbourhood.

If your dog wants to spend five minutes sniffing around one particular area, that's their choice for this activity. If you feel frustrated, try to remember how sensitive your dog's nose is and that they are finding out who has passed by this spot and when. It's like the dog version of checking their newsfeed or social media. Having this opportunity can significantly contribute to your dog's quality of life. When there is a choice of direction, you can use a cue such as 'which way?', to let your dog decide which option appeals to them most.

TOP TRAINING TIPS

🐾 Bring on the challenge! If your dog is still keen on being more mentally active, you can build some additional activities into your sniffy walks. For example, you might build in search games if you have already taught your dog this concept at home; you might hide a toy you've brought with you or drop your keychain and then ask your dog to go and find it. But make sure you know where your keys are and that your dog is competent at searching first! Some people use treats while on walks but you should be cautious about encouraging your dog to eat things they find unless you know it's a safe area where it is unlikely that they will consume leftover takeaway meals or other dangerous items.

🐾 The main challenge in this game is for you to be the perfectly patient partner – go on, you might find you enjoy taking things a bit more slowly too!

MUFFIN TRAY CHALLENGE

WHAT YOU'LL NEED
- A muffin baking tray
- A range of balls that fit into the tray
- Some tasty treats

Get ready

Set the muffin tray in a location where your dog can comfortably access it. If your dog has mobility issues, this might be on the floor in front of them, or set on a footstool or box to raise it up from the floor to avoid them having to bend over. Consider your dog and their own physical requirements for this game.

Get steady

Place some treats into the muffin tray and then position balls over the top. If it helps to get your dog's enthusiasm up, let them see you preparing the tray.

Let's play!

Encourage your dog to find the treats. They are likely to be able to smell the treats, or have at least watched you hide them, so now they need to learn that they have to lift the balls out one by one in order to access what is hidden underneath. Praise them when they succeed.

TOP TRAINING TIPS

🐾 If your oldie is struggling, make sure that the position of the tray is suitable. Start by placing some treats into the tray without covering them up so that your dog learns that goodies can be found in this location. Next, hide one treat under a ball and encourage your dog to work out how to remove it to access the treats. Build up the difficulty as their confidence grows.

🐾 Bring on the challenge! Now you can hide treats under just some of the balls. Your dog will either have to take time to sniff out the locations of the treats, or be persistent and lift out all the balls to check.

STEP UP

WHAT YOU'LL NEED
- A sturdy box or a footstool (size depends on your dog)
- Treats

Get ready

Start this game by selecting a raised platform or surface that is stable, secure, and safe for your dog to step onto. It could be a low step, a sturdy box, or a specially designed dog-training platform. You might start low and work up to higher options later.

Get steady

Position yourself so that you are beside or in front of the step, with your dog on the other side. Using a treat in your hand, get your dog's attention.

Let's play!

Lure your dog towards the step with the treat by moving it over the raised surface. Your aim is to encourage them to follow and step up in order to reach the treat, their front paws being on the platform. Be quick with the reward before your dog hops up completely.

Repeat several times so that your dog becomes used to moving into position. When they get it right you can mark the behaviour with a 'yes' or a click, and then toss the treat away from the step so that they have to reset and approach it again for the next round of practice.

Add in your verbal cue, 'step up', as your dog moves into position. Remember to reward them each time to encourage the response.

The next task is to fade out the reliance on the lure. Use your verbal cue, 'step up', and gesture to the step as you have done before, but without holding the treat. Be ready to praise and reward them for responding by offering a treat from your pouch once they are in position.

Now you can start to practise in different locations, on new surfaces, possibly at varied heights. Build in some distractions too, to increase the likelihood of them responding in a real-life situation.

TOP TRAINING TIPS

🐾 Build up the duration of the step-up position by pausing before offering the praise and treat. Gradually increase this so that your dog can hold the position.

🐾 Bring on the challenge! You can use this position if you need your dog to be a little higher while you clip on their lead or harness, or while checking eyes and ears. Build these checks slowly into the routine so that your dog is always comfortable.

MOVE TO THE MIDDLE

Teaching your dog to come and stand between your legs can be a useful command for various reasons, such as keeping them close in a busy environment or as a starting base for more advanced tricks. For older dogs you might use this when you sense they are feeling a little overwhelmed or if you are worried that they might be bumped or knocked as people pass by.

WHAT YOU'LL NEED
- A selection of treats

Get ready

Choose a cue word for this action such as 'between', 'middle' or 'centre'. Be consistent with this cue throughout the training.

Get steady

Begin in a location that is free from distractions to make the lesson as easy as possible.

Let's play!

Hold a treat in your hand and get your dog's attention. Stand with your legs a bit wider than shoulder-width apart so that there's enough space for your dog to comfortably stand between them.

Let your dog see the treat in your hand. Encourage them to step behind you – toss a treat onto the floor to get them to move if necessary. Then hold another treat between your legs so that as they approach you, they move through from behind. Release the treat when they are between your legs.

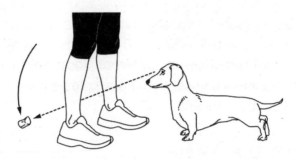

Reset the position by throwing another treat away to the side and starting again. If your dog approaches from the front, encourage them around but do not reward them for moving between your legs from the front.

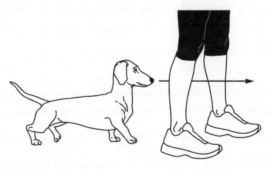

Start to introduce your verbal cue as your dog moves into the space between your legs. Always mark the moment and release the treat in this position.

Fade out the treat lure by encouraging your dog to move between your legs without the treat in your hand. Your stance, the cue and a hand gesture should be enough to get them trying initially and ensure that as soon as they are in place you give your marker ('yes' or click) and reward them.

Start to practise in different locations such as different rooms and on a quiet walk, to help your dog to generalize the concept.

TOP TRAINING TIPS

🐾 Build the duration of the 'between' position by pausing before the marker and reward are offered. Gradually build this up so that your dog is relaxed while standing between your legs for a duration that becomes useful in real-life scenarios.

🐾 Once your dog is responding well to this cue, start to introduce it in busy situations such as when people are passing by or when waiting in line.

🐾 Bring on the challenge! You might find it useful to teach your dog to walk forwards while remaining between your legs. Begin with one step at a time, going back to luring your dog to get them stepping with you. Once this is working well, introduce a cue such as 'forwards' to indicate that you are going to move. As before, fade out the lure and build up to greater distances as your dog learns the routine.

YOGA DOG

Teaching your dog a canine yoga game can be a wonderful way to bond, improve their flexibility and provide mental stimulation. It can be a lovely, relaxing activity compared to some of the more challenging or varied games for those wanting more. Some of the benefits from dog yoga have been likened to those that we experience, including supporting relaxation and stress reduction and providing a gentle exercise and stretching option.

WHAT YOU'LL NEED
- A non-slip mat or blanket for your dog (and one for you too)

Get ready

Set up a comfortable and quiet area in your home or backyard where you and your dog can practise canine yoga. Choose a time when your dog is relaxed and not overly excited. Consider ways to create a calm atmosphere, perhaps by dimming the lights, playing soothing music or using aromatherapy. It's important for both you and your dog to be in a calm state of mind.

Get steady

The positions you bring into this activity can involve many of the foundation actions in Start With the Basics (page 65) and some of the other games in this book. However, they should be performed slowly and steadily and combined to suit the needs of your dog.

Let's play!

Choose the poses that seem appropriate for you and your dog's shape and physical ability. As with human yoga, this should only be performed if your dog is physically well enough to perform the movements. If in doubt, discuss with your vet.

Puppy pose

This is the play 'bow' position that your dog will instinctively display when they are feeling playful. Observe your dog during their play sessions and when they naturally perform this playful bow, use your chosen verbal cue, such as 'bow', and immediately reward them with praise and treats. This helps them associate the cue with the behaviour.

Begin with your dog in a standing position, hold a treat to their nose and lure them downwards to the floor. As they drop their head, give your verbal cue 'bow' and reward them. Be quick with your timing since if you delay your dog might drop their whole body down. Continue to practise and build up the duration of the pose.

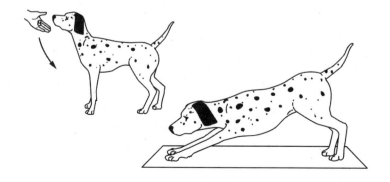

Upward-facing dog

You can modify the human pose to suit your dog. Begin by encouraging them into a down position. Lure them upwards by holding a treat to their nose and slowly moving it upwards so that they stretch up, reaching upwards with their neck extended. If your dog starts to rise part way up on their front paws, this is perfect, but modify the movement to suit their abilities. You can give a consistent verbal cue, 'stretch', or a hand signal to encourage this pose. For example, you can use an open-palm gesture to signal your dog to lift their chest. Pair this up with the pose so that the gesture has meaning for them. Always remember to praise and reward your dog for their attempts. Yoga celebrates all effort and recognizes that differing body shapes will alter the pose for each individual.

Now add in the various poses and actions already included in this book: roll over (page 202), belly-up (page 223), wave (page 126), look left and look right (page 211), and build on these actions with your imagination. As with all the poses, incremental lifts, stretches or bends can be built in over time.

TOP TRAINING TIPS

🐾 Take your time to sit and breathe with your dog before you begin your sessions. Being calm and relaxed will influence your dog positively too.

🐾 Bring on the challenge! Some dogs are so comfortable with their owners that they can be involved with more advanced poses, including balancing on you or being lifted with you as part of a duo yoga session.

TUMBLING TOWERS

This easy game is entertaining for older dogs who are less able to be physically active, but is also a wonderful game to use while building up the confidence of more sensitive dogs. It is often a way to build in tolerance to movement and noises, and can be as gentle and quiet as you like, or involve more clattering and banging for those dogs who enjoy such things.

WHAT YOU'LL NEED

- Treats
- A set of plastic toddler stacking cups or several cardboard inserts, paper cups
- Spoons, keys, or other noisy items including empty drinks cans
- A towel

Get ready

Consider your dog carefully. Are they sensitive and easily startled? No game should ever cause alarm or fear, so it is very important that you take this one steadily and avoid any set-up that might worry your dog. If you are unsure, start with the easier stages and then, with each change, observe very carefully and decide what is an appropriate level for them.

Get steady

While your dog is placed out of the room, or is watching from a distance, stack the plastic cups with a treat placed

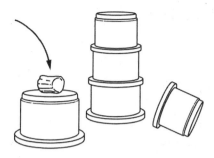

between each layer. Doing this on a carpeted area or on a towel will make it a nice quiet game until your dog gets the idea. If your dog is very sensitive, begin with just two cups and build up as they find their confidence.

Let's play!

Encourage your dog to come forward to explore the cups. They are likely to sniff and nudge the tower, causing it to topple. Doing so releases the treats. All dogs, whether they have mobility or eyesight problems, can enjoy this activity. Let them snuffle about and eat the treats before you ask them to sit and reset again.

Some dogs will stay on this level, growing less worried about the movement they cause as the cups topple and the muffled noises of the plastic bouncing

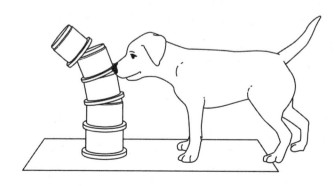

on the carpet or towel. Highly sensitive dogs can topple towers made from cardboard inner rolls or paper cups, which are quieter when knocked over but no less fun to forage among.

Progression with this game can come in the form of making a taller tower, or creating one with slightly higher levels of noise once it falls. Each dog will be unique, so take your time and never rush this part. Depending on the size of your dog and the stacking cups, you might be able to hide a ball or small toy in there, though for most dogs treats will be the safer option (balls that are too small pose a choking danger). However, a favourite toy could be balanced on top.

TOP TRAINING TIPS

Adding in noisy components to this game aims to build your dog's tolerance to sudden sounds. Giving your dog control over knocking down the tower and thus creating the sound themselves affords a predictable aspect to the game, and the sound, followed by delicious treats on the floor, will help your dog to associate the noisy event with the arrival of food, leading them to automatically respond as if food is arriving when they hear sudden sounds in future. This creates protection against a fear response developing instead. Dogs who are already sensitive can be very gently exposed to sounds and some positive associations created to support a bigger, more detailed training programme.

Examples for adding complexity to this game include: balancing a spoon on top of the tower, hiding keys inside one of the cups, adding an empty drink can, building up the number of cans so that the noise increases as they fall. Always do this on soft carpeting or a towel until you know that your dog is feeling happy and confident.

Bring on the challenge! If your dog is bounding into the tower, wagging and showing no signs of flinching as it falls, you may want to progress to a smaller towel and gradually onto a hard floor where the sound will be louder. Always hide the treats in the tower so that your dog is rewarded for participating and for ignoring the noise.

ACKNOWLEDGEMENTS

Thank you to all the wonderful dogs and their owners who inspire me with their efforts every day. Heartfelt thanks to my husband and son who were so supportive during my many late nights spent typing, and of course a nod to my cheeky dogs who keep me on my toes.

ABOUT THE AUTHOR

Claire Arrowsmith (BSc (Hons) MSc CCAB) is a Certified Clinical Animal Behaviourist and Principal Practitioner for the Pet Behaviour Centre, where she helps dogs and cats with behavioural problems. She is a Full Member of the Association of Pet Behaviour Counsellors and Fellowship of Animal Behaviour Clinicians. She has worked with problem behaviour cases since graduating with a Masters in Applied Animal Behaviour and Animal Welfare from Edinburgh University in 2000. She divides her time between running the Pet Behaviour Centre, acting as a Visiting Lecturer on the Clinical Animal Behaviour degree course at Harper Adams University and supporting a local police force with canine behavioural guidance. She is the author of *Brain Games for Dogs, Correcting Bad Habits in Dogs* and *Instant Dog Training*.